"Regardless of the challenges we fa
ability to overcome. It just requires c
tion. And I can assure you the inform
mation for how to raise your teenager.

Jimmy Evans
Founder and CEO, MarriageToday

"As a mentor to young adults and a father, I am very thankful for Candy's insight and expertise with teens. Parents today are wading through an extremely different culture that has a skewed worldview. Rescue *has provided them with a unique vantage point that will help them decipher truth amidst the lies."*

Brandon Slay
2000 Olympic Gold Medalist, Freestyle Wrestling
National Development Coach

"For years Candy's compassion and insights have been a life line for families across the country. Rescue *is where the 'rubber meets the road.' Real insights from real teens...a must read for every parent."*

Dr. Scott Sticksel
Co-founder, The BridgeWorks Group LLC

"Candy has truly thrown us a life preserver! And through the time she spent with the Lifeguards, she now draws us nearer to the One Who Saves. Dive in!"

Teri Hollis
Author of seeGODseeGOOD series

"Candy is a passionate crusader who has committed her life to throwing out life preservers to young people and families in crisis. Candy's gift of communication empowers her to be highly effective in reaching teens and parents alike."

Kim Witcher
Women's Pastor, Trinity Fellowship Church

"Preparing our children to navigate the seas of life is a challenging task for all parents. It is made even more difficult when the storms of life create turbulent waves. Candy provides guidance and encouragement for all parents of teens navigating the transitional waters to adulthood. This book is a must read!"

Tom Lane
Executive Senior Pastor Gateway Church

Author of *The Influence of a Father*

Rescue

Raising Teens in a Drowning Culture

CANDY GIBBS

All examples involving ministry situations are real. However, the details and surrounding the circumstances may have been altered or combined to preserve the privacy and confidentiality of the individuals involved.

Fedd Books
Post Office Box 341973
Austin, TX 78734
www.thefeddagency.com

Published in association with the literary agency of The Fedd Agency, Inc.

Editing by A.J. Gregory and Layce Smith
Cover and Interior Design by Mitchell Shea

Printed in the United States of America
First Edition 2014

ISBN: 978-0-9894934-5-1
eISBN: 978-0-9894934-7-5

For Jake and Madi:

Thank you for dealing with this mom as your lifeguard. I am so honored to swim alongside you, and the biggest joy of my life is watching you catch a wave of His Presence. You are my inspiration. Swim for all your worth! "Deep calls to deep..." (Psalm 42:7)

I love you,

Mom

Contents

Acknowledgments

Reach down your hand from on high; deliver me and rescue me from the mighty waters...

Psalm 144: 7

CareNet staff and Board of Directors, thank you so much for your support and prayers. It is truly my privilege to serve with you. Rescue required much time and emotion and without you, we would have surely drowned.

Provenance Consulting, you are amazing and we will never be able to thank you enough. You have given life to a vision from the Father to impact our culture for the Kingdom. I am forever grateful.

Amy Powell, thank you for using your incredible gift of grace and organization to make our filming weekend happen so smoothly.

Christy Hilbert, I love your passionate pursuit of the Father. Thank you for helping me to communicate with the Lifeguards and for loving so many so well.

Rick and Brenda Trafton, thank you for sharing your retreat with me and for loving me and my family. I love you so and your life is an outflow of your intimate worship of our God. I humbly thank you.

Whitney Gossett, you are the most professional, diplomatic, adorable young woman, and I am better for working with you. You are such a gift.

Ana Hoeksema, the Lord has simply yoked us together. Thank you for encouraging when I thought I'd quit and believing when I could not. We made it! Love you.

All you other prayer warriors (you know who you are), you cannot know what strength and peace came to us through your pouring out your heart to the Father on our behalf. We felt as if we were carried on a wave of His Presence. Thank you.

Fedd Books, I am so grateful for your patience, encouragement, and expertise. Great job!

Matt Rowley, thank you for staying the course. I am always honored to serve with you, my friend.

Pastor Jimmy Evans, thank you for your prayers and for always standing with us. You are always on His side and for that I am so grateful. You are a treasured friend.

Lifeguards, because I believe in you and in His Spirit who is alive and active in you, this project is a reality. You prayed for me. You encouraged me. You literally lead the way as we swam these uncharted seas. You are the real deal, and I love each of you. I am always in your corner. Struggle well.

Brian Gibbs, we have done it again. You are the visionary and courage of this outfit. Thank you for dealing with my late nights of writing and early mornings in tears. Without you, I would not be me. I love you. You speak peace to the storms and hope in the midst of chaos. You are the best.

Tanner, the last time I wrote an acknowledgement for you I said, “Be a great man of God.” While working on this project you became a United States Airman. I am so proud of you and Whitney. I love you, Nerd Face.

Jake, you are a leader and I love you. Thank you for believing in me and what He has called our family to, you amaze me. I pray peace and adventure for you as you swim the waves with Him. I am proud to be your mom. 4.

Madison, you are a joy and delight and I am so thankful the Lord gave me you. You are a beautiful balance of strength and grace. You see people for who they are. I am honored to be your mom. I love you, Madio.

Lord Jesus, I am thankful that You are sure footed on the roughest seas, and when we turn our gaze toward You, You calm our storms. I love You more than I can ever express. Thank You for loving me first. You are truly my Rescue.

I am so honored to have experienced this journey with each of you!

Candy

Foreword

My wife, Karen, and I have been called to minister to marriages. At the heart of what we do is to help couples overcome the challenges that could threaten their marital satisfaction and even lead to divorce. But even more, we help couples thrive in intimate, secure relationships. What we do is very rewarding and, in the world we live in, it is in high demand.

In writing books and teaching on marriage over the years I have done a lot of research on the dynamics of family and marriage. One of the things I discovered many years ago is that the most stressful season for most married couples is when they are parenting teenagers.

Karen and I can attest to it. Our children are now grown and have children of their own. But back in the season when our children were teens it was non-stop drama. Our daughter, Julie, is three years older than our son, Brent. Between them we were constantly dealing with the issues of puberty, attitudes, friends, school, boundaries, curfews, sex, dating, and so on.

Even though we had a good marriage that survived those years, it was challenging. And at times we found ourselves exhausted, discouraged, confused, and even divided. But by God's grace we fought and prayed our way through it and decided not to give up and not to allow the issues our children were going through to divide.

But, having said all of that, let me add one very important thing: We did it in a different world than now. With all of the challenges we faced, today's world is much different and much more dangerous. We parented before there were cell phones or the Internet. We parented when society was much more respectful of authority and much less tolerant of rebellion.

We parented when it was still considered wrong for teens to have sex before marriage. We parented when you could assume that teachers and other parents shared your same values. In other words, we parented in a much different world than today.

Karen and I now have five grandchildren ranging in ages from eight months to twelve years old. Our twin granddaughters will turn thirteen next year, officially making them teenagers. And they will navigate their teen years in this new world. And our daughter, Julie, and her husband, Cory, will have to face the unique challenges of raising teenagers in this age of rebellion, immorality, and ungodliness.

But in spite of this, I know they can and will succeed. Regardless of the challenges we face in life, God always gives us the ability to overcome. It just requires commitment and the right information. And I can assure you the information in this book is the right information for how to raise your teenager.

I have known Candy Gibbs for many years. She is truly an expert on raising teenagers. She has done a stellar job of heading the CareNet Crisis Pregnancy Center in our community. Every day she deals with teenagers and their parents. And every day she sees the reality of what is happening in the real world and the consequences.

In addition, Candy has three children of her own. In this book she describes how she and her husband deal with the real and modern challenges of raising their teens. And as I have read this book, I couldn't agree with her more. Candy shares more than information, she shares wisdom that comes from years of experience and doing things right.

If there has ever been a world that needed this book, it is ours. And if there has ever been a person qualified to write it, it is Candy. I so wish there would have been a resource like this when our children were younger. But I am so glad I will be able to give copies of this book to my children to equip them to raise our grandchildren.

Jimmy Evans
Founder and CEO

MarriageToday

Becoming a Rescue Swimmer
(aka an effective Parent of a Teen)

"According to the Rescue Swimmer course syllabus, rescue swimmers must have flexibility, strength and endurance, and be able to function for 30 minutes in heavy seas. So, being comfortable in the water is an understatement. You have to be able to think and perform challenging tasks while submerged, holding your breath, and getting tossed around by 10 to 20 foot waves.

Rescue swimmers also must have the skills to provide basic pre-hospital life support for rescued individuals. And as part of their training, candidates must complete an emergency medical training (EMT) course. This is not an ordinary EMT – exposed to high seas, rough terrain, and other dangers and ordinary EMT will not survive.

The training you are seeking is hardcore physical and mental training that will challenge you to your core. In fact, Rescue Swimmer School boasts more than a 50% attrition rate – so it is crucial for you to go to the training scoring high in your PFT (personal fitness test), but more importantly – be confident in the water. Not cocky! You must have a deep respect for the power of the sea, but know that your training will help save your life and the lives of the ocean's victims."[1]

This direct quote above, taken from www.military.com, describes the grueling task of becoming a Rescue Swimmer in the United States Coast Guard. After reading that, how many of us thought it might be the job description for parenting teenagers in the twenty-first century?

Rescue swimmers must have flexibility, strength, endurance, and...be able to think and perform challenging tasks while submerged...

Flexibility can mean a multitude of things to the parent of a teenager. You must maintain a flexible schedule, sometimes "going with the flow." You may need to run money to the school before lunch to cover the cost of that field trip they've known about for two weeks and forgot to mention. Or you may need to make a spur of the moment run to the mall to get new pants for the band concert (The khakis you bought three weeks ago are now three inches too short.). Flexibility could mean "going with the flow." When you asked your daughter to pick up her room, you thought it might happen before dinner; she thought you meant sometime before she leaves for college. Flexibility could mean whipping up dinner for the baseball team in the next fifteen minutes so they can eat before practice. Flexibility is as necessary for the parent of teens as a cape to Superman.

Strength is a pre-requisite for parenting teens. Well, you could simultaneously acquire it in the process, but one way or the other you will be able to win the World's Strongest Man (or Woman) competition on the other side of it! You have to be strong enough to sit through a five-hour awards assembly to see your child's three seconds of fame, and you have to be strong enough to cheer with enthusiasm when their competition's name is announced instead. You have to be strong enough to lift a fifty-pound backpack in the middle of the night after breaking your pinky toe on it. You have to be strong enough to stay up into the wee hours of the morning praying for your son and strong enough to finally lay it at God's feet and go to sleep. You have to be strong enough to lift six grocery-filled bags at once, two dogs the kids forgot to let in for the night, and four loads of smelly laundry that need to be taken to the laundry room. You also must be strong enough to discuss drugs, sex, integrity, suicide, and faith while being honest and vulnerable. You have to be strong enough to hang on for dear life and strong enough to let go. Parenting teens isn't for the weak in the knees or the faint of heart.

Endurance. Love endures all things, right? As the parent of a teen you will endure many things. You will endure several last minute projects. Moms who have daughters, you will endure never being able to locate your favorite shoes or earrings until you spot them on your daughter's friend from down the street. You'll endure trying to get red baseball field dirt out of your son's white baseball pants over a million times. You will endure constant aggravating and arguing amongst your children, and then you will endure the unexplained, instantaneous shift to full-on belly laughing. You will endure wins, losses, failures, and successes. You will endure those seven years between the ages of thirteen and nineteen, and just about the time you think you can't take it for another moment, they will walk across the high school graduation stage, and all of a sudden you realize you would endure it all again for a few nights on the front porch or a long walk at the park with them.

Flexibility, strength, and endurance—I'd say so.

Must...be able to function for 30 minutes in heavy seas. So, being comfortable in the water is an understatement. You have to be able to think and perform challenging tasks while submerged, holding your breath, and getting tossed around by 10-20 ft. waves.

Now we are getting to it—the reason I decided to write the book. As the parent of a teenager (or more than one), you will have to be able to function in heavy seas. You will be submerged, required to hold your breath at times, and you will be tossed around by twenty-foot waves.

I have been married to my husband, Brian, for sixteen years. Tanner, our oldest, was only five years old when Brian and I married. I learned so much going from having no children to being the stepmother of a precious, full-of-life, five-year-old and working through the intricacies of a blended family. Tanner is now married to our daughter-in-law, Whitney, and we have a precious grandson, Bracen, and a brand new granddaughter, Bayler! Brian and I also have two teenagers, a son, Jake and, a daughter, Madison. All of that to say, we have been through or are currently in the stages you are living. I know sometimes it truly feels like drowning.

One normal afternoon changed my life. I was working diligently on something, and I am sure it was extremely important, when our receptionist came in and asked if I could visit with a family that had come in. I walked up front and there stood four precious adults. Both the dad and the granddad were farmers and "guy's guys"—tall and strong from doing what the Lord had called them to do. The mom and the grandmother were absolutely adorable, and I fell in love with all of them immediately. All four were there looking for a life preserver.

The younger couple had a teenage daughter who was literally being pulled under, actively drowning, in her culture. The father was an active, well-known, and respected man in their small community, and their daughter had nude photos of herself shared via a cell phone by the young man she was dating, a young man her family did not approve of. The daughter had also recently found out she was pregnant. This family needed a lifeguard and they need one now.

I will never forget the look in that hurting daddy's eyes as he asked, "Can you help us?"

I replied, "If you can get her here, we will help her, because *He* will be here waiting."

A few days passed and in came the receptionist again. This time her eyes were as big as saucers as she said, "We need you up front." When I walked into the waiting room, I saw the most beautiful young woman sobbing in a chair and that same sweet daddy with tears streaming down his face.

"You said if we got her here, you would help us." Turns out that sweet, desperate daddy had literally picked up his half-drowned daughter off the floor of her closet, loaded her up, and brought her to "shore," so to speak.

How did they get here? I could almost read his mind, one parent's heart to another. I could see images of her birth, of her running through fields of flowers, and of her rushing to be first in line for the slide. I could see her in dance recitals and being baptized. I could see her playing sports and receiving awards at school. I could see her potential. I could see her warm and dry, skipping along the beach. But I could also see her brokenness. I saw her drenched in shame, regret, and poor choices in the midst of heavy seas with a society whose undertow words cannot describe. I saw them.

But I saw God too.

> A furious squall came up, and the waves broke over the boat, so that it was nearly swamped. Jesus was in the stern, sleeping on a cushion. The disciples woke him and said to him, "Teacher, don't you care if we drown?" He got up, rebuked the wind and said to the waves, "Quiet! Be still!" Then the wind died down and it was completely calm. He said to his disciples, "Why are you so afraid? Do you still have no faith?" They were terrified and asked each other, "Who is this? Even the wind and the waves obey him!"
>
> Mark 4:37-41

Even the winds and the waves obey Him! I'll tell you something else, those disciples who witnessed Jesus command a raging sea to be silent and still; they know a little something about trusting Him in the storms. Those who have been saved from high seas understand the importance of a lifeguard.

So, I decided to find us some lifeguards—young men and women who have seen rough waters and smooth sailing; young adults who have seen Him walking out to them on the water and who, at other times, had to swim with all they had to reach the shore. Lifeguards who have sailed these seas can give us much needed insight into the storms we face.

This process began many months ago with a simple idea. My husband and I were discussing current culture and all of the new unique issues our teens are facing. As we talked, faces of young adults, mostly college age, raced through my mind. Some of them struggled as they maneuvered through junior high and high school experiences, and some of them literally seemed to grow stronger and stronger as they were faced with challenges and overcame them. Thus, the vision for this book was birthed.

What if we spent time with each of those types of young people and asked them for their perspective on growing up in today's culture? Would we get the responses that we, as parents and mentors, expect? Or would it be something completely different?

As you embark on this journey with us, I can promise that at points you will feel validated in the stances you've taken with your own children and or perhaps challenged to take a new stand. You will also be blown away at times by the insight, discussion, and answers this amazing group of Lifeguards provide.

This book is written using material gathered over an eighteen-month period spent in live chat with a group of fourteen college students. These young people come from different backgrounds and were raised by parents with differing sets of value. During the eighteen months in which we worked together, I would submit a topic or a question to the group and they would respond based on their own experience. We talked about many things, and I have divided up the discussions I found most insightful into chapters.

I can so sympathize with you as a parent and asked the group questions I believe will benefit all of us. Because I am certain the truth of God's Word is all that we have to base our lives on, I will be sharing a Biblical perspective throughout. As you dig through this book, you will find the chapters broken up as follows:

- **Commentaries from me**—written from my perspective and experience as a mother of three children, including two teenagers, and as the Executive Director of CareNet Pregnancy Centers in Amarillo, Texas. I have counseled many parents who are stuck in difficult situations and rejoiced with those who have swam through the murky waters and raging seas of parenting teens.

- **Let's Ask the Lifeguards**—commentary from the young people we have chosen to offer their advice and share their experience based on specific, posed questions. The thoughts from our Lifeguards are verbatim so you can get a sense of each Lifeguard's personality. While I do not always share their opinions, I felt it important for you to glimpse inside the heart of these young people. (The bios I have included will help give you little background with their varying responses.

- **Treading Tips**—practical nuggets of wisdom summarize the lessons and perspective for each topic.

- **Life Preservers**—relevant and encouraging Scripture.

As we begin this journey together, I want to encourage you in your parenting. No one knows your children like you do. No one loves them as much, sees the truth in their eyes, and is concerned with the details of their lives like you. We have all made mistakes as parents and have things we would have done differently, looking back.

The material we offer in this book is meant to encourage, challenge, and teach you about the sometimes-difficult stage of parenting teenagers in light of today's culture. It is my hope that you will understand my heart, the heart of the Lifeguards, and mostly the heart of the Father toward your teen while we address relevant issues. As I have said, parenting through the teenage years can be a tumultuous time of swimming against society, but it can also be a time of great joy. Don't give up and settle for less than what the Lord has in mind for your teen. One thing that is so important for our generation to remember is that our actions, the way we live our lives, is the best example for our children.

I'd rather see a sermon than hear one any day,
I'd rather one should walk with me than merely tell the way.
The eye's a better pupil and more willing than the ear,
Fine counsel is confusing, but example's always clear;
And the best of all the preachers are the men who live their creeds,
For to see the good in action is what everybody needs.

I can soon learn how to do it if you'll let me see it done;
I can watch your hands in action, but your tongue too fast may run.

And the lectures you deliver may be very wise and true,
But I'd rather get my lesson by observing what you do;
For I might misunderstand you and the high advice you give,
But there's no misunderstanding how you act and how you live.
Edgar A. Guest "Sermons We See"

Oh, and finally, I don't want to leave our young woman and her daddy soaked in shame in the waiting room of our office, because that is certainly not where she ended up. After lots of hard swimming, some days gaining ground and some days losing a little, she went on to graduate from a major Christian university with a degree in education. She is married to the love of her life and just gave birth to a beautiful baby girl! Her parents, they had some tough days—that sea salt can sure sting your eyes. But today, they are glowing grandparents who would beckon you from their spot on the shore, "Keep swimming! You've almost made it!"

My heart is so full of anxious anticipation for what the Lord may show you through my time with this amazing group of young people.

Are you ready to dive in with me?

Meet the Lifeguards

Jace is majoring in communications and business at Cornell University, where he is a collegiate wrestler. He plans to attend law school after graduation. Jace is passionate about wrestling, hunting, and Jesus.

Layne has an early childhood education degree from Texas Tech University. She married Justin in December of 2012 and is a first grade teacher in Amarillo, Texas. Her passion is to have a family and continue her work with kids. Her favorite movie quote is, "Your life is an occasion, rise to it," from *Mr. Magorium's Wonder Emporium*. Layne says, "God has us here for a purpose and we are called to be intentional and not sit back and let life pass us by."

Matt graduated from Lubbock Christian University, where he played four years of collegiate baseball, with a bachelors degree in youth and family ministry. He is a youth pastor in Panhandle, Texas, and was married in June of 2014. If Matt could spend a day with anyone it would be the Greek philosopher, Aristotle.

Stephanie is majoring in nursing at Montana State University. Growing up in a family with three sisters, Stephanie believes her biggest strengths are her relational skills—I'd say so! One of Stephanie's favorite movie quotes is, "Sooner or later you're going to realize just as I did that there's a difference between knowing the path and walking the path," from *The Matrix*.

Andrew graduated in 2014 from Oklahoma State University. He is married to Peyton and is preparing for medical school. He believes God has called him into the medical field. Andrew says scripture memory is the most important thing to him. He says, "the Word of God is our sword. We must hide it in our hearts."

Luke recently graduated with honors from the University of Texas at Austin with a bachelor of science in radio-television-film. He is on the promotional-materials team for South by Southwest Music-Film-Interactive Conferences, has been a production assistant for the feature film *The Black Rider*, and plans to attend the American Academy of Dramatic Arts in Los Angeles.

Paris graduated from the University of North Texas with a bachelor of arts in interdisciplinary studies and a minor in religious studies. As the older sister to three younger brothers, Paris believes God has a big family of her own in her future. She is passionate about family ministry.

Stefanie graduated with a bachelor of arts degree in interdisciplinary studies from Texas A&M University after spending one year at a ministry school in California. She hopes to pursue a master's degree in speech and language pathology and become a speech therapist for children. Stephanie hopes to start a clean water ministry and work with victims of sex trafficking some day. She has a heart for seeing God's power set people free. Amen to that!

Tate is majoring in sports and exercise at West Texas A&M University. He plans to teach and coach in a high school. Tate's favorite verse is Psalm 144:1: "God has trained us and is preparing us for whatever may be thrown at us, and when trial comes we will be ready as long as we trust our God." He says he applies this verse to sports and to life.

Theresa graduated with a bachelor's degree in music theater from Oklahoma City University. She has recently been selected to represent her school in the NYC showcase in hopes of landing some roles on Broadway! She plans to move to New York and minister through music and share God's love through her voice. Most of us would be scared to death, but Theresa says there is nothing like being on stage, with a huge orchestra underfoot, singing for an audience. Wow.

Kaylee has her bachelor's degree in social work with a minor in marriage and family counseling from Southwestern Assemblies of God University in Waxahachie, TX. Currently, she is working at the University of Texas in Arlington and attending classes for her master's degree in social work. She spends her free time volunteering with the Make-A-Wish Foundation—a real dream come true for her!

Christian is majoring in accounting and prelaw at Texas A&M University. Christian also volunteers with Living Water International. If she could spend a day with anyone, it would be her grandfather. Christian loves to sit at the piano and play and write music until her head clears. She has three sisters and two precious nephews that she says have given her a glimpse into what "take a bullet for you" kind of love is.

Your Family

The family is important, and it is necessary for the survival of humanity. Without the family, the cultural survival of the human race would be at risk. The family, whether we like it or not, is the foundation.
Pope Francis

When my sister and I can, we love to take our kids on a trip during spring break. We were in Oklahoma City a few years ago and had just wrapped up a super-fun-packed day with our kids. They had eaten, swam, showered, and were finally tucked away for the night. About midnight, Cara and I were watching a movie when I received a text from one of my dear friends. When I think back on it, I don't know if I realized at the time what a pivotal moment that was. Sometimes one discovery, a twelve-hour period, a minute time slot for that matter, can literally change the course of a family forever. This was that moment.

My friend had just discovered that her husband, dad to their three sons, was having an affair with one of her friends and planned to leave her. Our oldest son and theirs grew up together; my youngest, Madi, and their youngest son are the same age; and our middles, though two years apart, were best buds. I am not blaming either of the parents. I know both of them had struggles, fears, and wounds, as do we all. But everyone in that sweet family paid a price, because when the winds blew and the salt water began to fly, they needed the anchor to hold, and this time it didn't. They have all gone on with life, and I love when our paths cross—just wish things had turned out differently.

Our children and our teens need parental stability, the anchor, to hold. They need your marriage and family to stay committed to one another and strong in faith. When your children grasp for something to hold on to in the middle of a storm, they will reach for the anchor of your family.

Two of the most important topics that I discussed with the Lifeguards were marriage and family. In fact, so many of our topics led right back to this critical foundation. There are so many aspects to marriage and family (it is truly the groundwork of our society) that it was a daunting task for us to narrow down the topics. As I write this afternoon, I'm reading through all of the discussions that we had with the Lifeguards, and it's powerful.

Affection for Your Spouse

As Christian parents, we are doing some things well. Our young people appreciate things that they see in our marriages and some of the traditions that we've developed in our homes. That revelation brings me a great deal of hope and satisfaction! I believe that much of our discoveries about the hope our teens have in marriage and family will encourage you as well. Some of the Lifeguards said things like:

"My parents are best friends."

"My parents do everything together."

"They make decisions together."

"They are a team."

I especially love what one of our Lifeguards said: "My parents don't know how to quit on each other or on us. They have fought for their relationship. They talk through every different issue."

With the exception of one or two of the Lifeguards, each of these young men and women come from strong families, families who are committed to one another. Something I believe the church does well is to stress the order of priorities that the Lord has established. Our first priority should be Him, our second should be our family, and then third should be all of the other things (work, play, etc.).

My good friend, Pastor Jimmy Evans of Trinity Fellowship Church in Amarillo and president of Marriage and Family Today, wrote a book called, *7 Secrets of Successful Families*. He says, "Priorities demonstrate our value system as well as the value system we will pass on to our children."[2] The Lifeguards value the time their parents spend with them and the time their parents spend with one another. They value time spent talking, family vacations, and creating traditions, which builds security and establishes an anchor.

Something else I learned with the Lifeguards is that teenagers actually *like* to see their parents show affection toward each other. That makes me chuckle, because I know whenever Brian and I hug, kiss, or flirt with each other in our home, our kids will often laugh, gag, or make a silly comment. Even though romance or physical affection can sometimes be embarrassing and awkward, it brings your kids great security to see that the two of you are committed to and in love with one another. Continue to be affectionate as parents; it is important to your teens.

Paris said, "My parents are so in love and so expressive that I am now a romantic. I know what love looks like and when love is real." Another of the Lifeguards expressed that she wished her parents were more open about their love. Don't be afraid to express yourself and to be affectionate with each other. I wouldn't necessarily recommend giving slobbery kisses in front of your teens' friends, but it's ok to hold hands during a family move. Or, give your spouse a bear hug at the breakfast table before he or she leaves for work.

Let's ask the Lifeguards

What did you learn about marriage in your home?

My parents are so in love and it is so cool to see that. They are always dancing around the kitchen and holding hands and kissing. I am such a huge romantic, and growing up with that, I know how to pursue that. It is so encouraging. (Paris)

I learned a lot watching my parents fight for what they have. My siblings and I saw them fight and we saw them talk through issues and make hard decisions, and that was very important to me growing up. (Stephanie H.)

My parents are best friends. They aren't very romantic, but that really isn't their personality. If I had to say there was something I would like to be different...I would like them to be more affectionate. But they are definitely best friends and always support one another. (Kaylee)

My parents choose every day to be married. Every day they try to out-serve each other. It ends up in this hopelessly-deep love affair. It is the two of them and Jesus, and it is centered on Christ. If they didn't have that for the last twenty-nine years...that is why we are able to stay together. (Andrew)

My parents...they definitely don't know how to give up, and they have incorporated that in my life. I don't know how to quit because they never quit—not on each other and not on us kids. They are completely humble. I absolutely love watching them be married. They were next-door neighbors in second grade. (Jace)

My parents are still romantic and in love. I want to model my marriage after them. (Luke)

As you can see from the Lifeguards responses, the positive attributes that are modeled in a marriage now provide the groundwork for a child's future spouse and marriage. Our teenagers are watching the relationships we have with our spouses, and they pay attention to other couples' relationships around them. Teens can quickly decide whether this model of a relationship is something that they would like to imitate or avoid someday.

Keep in mind that allowing your teen to see that families and marriages are not perfect is a good thing; it brings an authentic reality. Because let's be honest, marriage can be difficult! That being said, it's also powerful to evidence a marriage grounded in Christ; this is what provides an anchor that can be trusted. When your own children are married and going through their own rough waters, it is important for them to have an example of marriage that has made it through the storm.

Many of the following comments from the Lifeguards are a mirror of what they have seen in their parent's relationship. Stefanie's parents are divorced, and she hasn't had a close relationship with her dad; thus, she is seeking a spouse who will fight for her. Andrew told us that his parents have faced difficult issues as a unit and with the guidance of Christ, so it isn't surprising that he sought a teammate. The relationships parents model set either a positive or negative standard.

What are you looking for in a spouse?

First, obviously, a good relationship with the Lord. But also fighting for me. Like, I think that is huge. I have a hard time trusting people. If someone would let me take my time, that would mean the world. (Stephanie P.)

I am a natural leader, so I am looking for someone who can match my boldness and be able to tell me no. His family has to come first and the way he treats his mom is important to me because that is how he will treat me. (Christian)

To have a woman so passionate about Christ that she puts

that relationship above ours. I need a woman that can challenge me and sharpen me. It may take a while for me to find that person. I need someone to be on my team because in this life we will run into all sorts of things. Third, you have to be attracted to each other. I mean she's got to be dime piece. (Andrew)

I am looking for a woman who has purpose in her life. I want her to have purpose more than just the average things. I want her to have purpose in what God wants her to do and something she has fun doing. I want her to be a good mom. My dad has told me you better find one who will be a good mom because you will love your kids more than anything. (Jace)

Here is a different perspective: Most women have probably made a list of the qualities they want in a husband, but if we look at it like I am—trying to become the woman I should be instead of focusing on the man so much—we would be more prepared to be who we should be. (Layne)

Affection for Your Child

It is beneficial for our children to see some form of affection exhibited by us as parents. However, they need to experience our affection for them as well. Both sons and daughters need to experience affection from their parents.

As our children hit puberty, their bodies begin to change, and even the most loving parents may begin to feel awkward and uncomfortable about expressing physical affection. Something I notice with my sons is that they will still hug me goodnight, let me sit next to them on the couch, and allow me to put my arm around them. Now, kissing them on the check before they get on the bus for a football game is out of the question, but they need affection, nonetheless.

Our daughters certainly need to receive physical affection and words of affirmation. Our daughters want to be beautiful and adored. I know that you want to be honoring and respectful, and I'm certainly not talking about anything less than that. I'm not talking about any kind of violation of her modesty. But girls still need healthy, physical affection not just from mom, but also from their dad. It fills her cup and helps her to understand that she is valuable. Girls need to be hugged and comforted by both parents. Laugh and cry together. Even in the most trying of times, sit by her on the couch. Put your arm around her and rub her hair. Kiss her on the cheek, and continue to express your love for her. Every young lady has a desire to be rescued. Until her knight comes, you're him.

While being beautiful and adored is important to most young ladies, being seen as strong and capable, being respected, is important to teen boys. As the mom of two sons, learning to relate to them strikes very close to home for me. I read John Eldridge's book, *Wild at Heart*, years ago. The book contains a section in which the author addresses the mother's role in her son's life.

> "Sometimes when the mother clings, he will try to tear himself away, violently. This typically comes in the teenage years and often involves some ugly behavior, maybe some foul words. She feels rejected, and he feels guilty, but he knows he must get away. This was my story, and my relationship with my mother has never been good since. I found that many, many adult men resent their mothers but cannot say why. They simply know they do not want to be close to them; they rarely call. As my friend David confessed, I hate calling my mom. She always says something like; 'it's so good to hear your little voice.'"

Something that has been difficult for me as a mother of two boys is to make the transition from babying them, to mothering them, to releasing them to be the young men God has called them to be. When communicate with our teenage sons, we need to accept them as young men, rather than our sweet little boy. Eldridge's book struck my heart because I do not want my sons to resent, avoid, or feel awkward around me.

The lessons I learned from the book acted like a rudder in my life to turn this huge ship 'round. At the time that I read *Wild at Heart*, my oldest son, Tanner, was about fourteen years old, and that would make my younger son, Jake, around seven. I want to have a strong relationship with all three of my children, but it comes more naturally with my daughter, simply because she's a girl and I get her.

Eldridge describes in his book that sons might feel as though they are betraying their mothers when they move on with their own lives. As mothers, we want to be an encouragement and support to our sons; we don't want to be the force that holds them back from their callings and aspirations or from their life partner, their wife.

My approach changed quickly. I now ask Tanner and Jake to open jars for me and to reach or fix things. I remind them how strong they are inside and out. I try really hard not to "baby" them, and I don't say things like, "You're just precious. I think you are darling." I try to tell them that I see the young men they are becoming and that I know the Lord has great and exciting plans for each of them.

Of course, when the boys became teenagers, I allowed Brian to be more of the disciplinarian when possible. Sure, I maintained a motherly role and definitely gave my opinion and disciplined when necessary. However, it was important for me to begin to allow them to become young men. I desire to approach them with respect to maintain a healthy relationship between us as they become adults. Learning to release them to become men of God and not feel some messed-up kind of guilt over it is important.

Obviously, my opinion is not to "baby" your daughter, nor to be unaffectionate with your son. Men have an inborn need to be respected. I believe we need to start building respect in our boys early. Likewise, women need love and affection, so parents should be a source of affection while young women are waiting for their spouse.

Sibling Relationships

Siblings. We love them yet want to eat their dessert and tattle on them all at the same time. I have one sister who is four years my junior, and she is a consistent fixture in a lifetime of memories. I have heard it said that siblings will likely be the longest relationship in a person's lifetime. When I remember the best memories of my life, my little sister is there, and I wouldn't have made it through the painful times of life without her. She is my best friend and the person most likely to be completely honest with me. She knows my quirks, my shoe size, my fears, my favorite color, and that I faint at the sight of blood. What would life be without our siblings?

A recurring theme in our discussion with the Lifeguards was the concept of a "golden child" and the "black sheep." As we talked, many of the lifeguards who felt like they were the golden children also felt they had a sibling who adopted the role of black sheep. One of the young men said, "I think the black sheep feels blacker when others are focused on the golden child." The same person also said they believe a sibling identifying themselves as the black sheep has a negative effect on the relationship. The group expressed that, even though they may be viewed as the golden child, they don't see themselves that way. They see and appreciate the talents and abilities of their siblings.

Let's Ask the Lifeguards

Are you the golden child? How does that affect your family?

In my family, my sisters would say that I am the golden child. They feel like my parents are giving me more attention than they are getting. I think that is ridiculous. That is not the way I see it. It is hard in those moments not to attack them. My parents have joked with each other that they have favorite children. I have to just walk away and not get mad. (Christian)

For me, I have been the front-runner in our family because I am the oldest and have been able to accomplish some things. When family and friends come over, they want to talk about the things I am doing, and I can tell it hurts my siblings' feelings. When I am alone with them, I focus on their talents. In public when people talk about me, I talk about them a lot so they don't feel insecure. My family and I are really good friends. (Jace)

As far as behavior goes, my sister is worlds ahead of me. My family is really close and we love each other and spend a lot of time together. But I do feel like the odd ball. Sometimes I look at pictures of me as a newborn to remind myself that I wasn't adopted, because I don't feel like I belong at home. My sister is so much more like my family, and I think they want me to be that way too, but they aren't going to say that. (Luke)

In high school I was the golden child. I had a lot of success and a lot of friends. A lot of friends didn't even know I had a sister and then knew her only as my sister. That really upset me because I felt like that was my fault. I didn't talk about my family and brag about my brother and sister. Now that I am out of high school, I feel like the roles have switched. I have had to really take a step back and let them have the glory, and that has been hard for me. (Tate)

It was important to the Lifeguards to be an encouragement to their siblings. The group felt it important that parents not compare their children. Each person had been uniquely gifted, and when comparisons are made between siblings, it often leads to hurt and wounded relationships.

It is important for us to allow our children to be different. Appreciating the strengths in each of them will help them to appreciate each other as well. The Bible tells us to train up a child in the way *he* should go...they each have their own journey to embark on, and it will not likely be the same path chosen by their brother or sister.

Peer Pressure can invade your family before you know it!

Peer pressure is such a big issue and so powerful. Parents naturally want their teens to fit in and not feel alienated. However, when we think rationally about peer pressure, and if you could see on a daily basis the situations that I see working with teens, then believe me, you *do* want them to be different.

Thinking back on my own adolescence, I did many things that I really didn't want to do; yet I did them because I didn't want to be the only one who didn't. I encourage you to think back about how powerful peer pressure was in your own life.

In my estimation, the early teen years may be one of the most difficult times in a young person's life. The name of the game is to make fun of someone before they have the chance to make fun of you. It is a very hostile environment. Teens oftentimes have some level of insecurity. They are trying to figure out who they are and camouflage their weaknesses while navigating eight hours a day that focus diligently on people's shortcomings or downfalls. It is a very difficult place; so, I would encourage *you* to be an encourager and a safe place. Our homes should be places of peace and of refuge. Learning as a mom to fight for peace in my home has been one of the most valuable lessons of my adult life.

It has become a common practice on my afternoon drive home to begin asking the Lord to come and be our peace, to leave the events of the day behind and focus fully on my family. I love 1 Corinthians 14:33, which says, "For God is not a God of disorder, but of peace." Peace is worth fighting for even in this "run as fast as you can, accomplish more than is humanly possible until you literally collapse in bed each night" society. Peace is critical. Our children need it and we need it.

This stage can be difficult because our young teens are only beginning to develop their moral compasses. Often times, they want to choose right, but they also so badly want to fit in. They are caught in the undertow of trying to please their parents and the Lord but still seem cool enough to hang out with their friends.

What is difficult is asking our teens to hold our convictions that have not yet become theirs. So, we simply set expectations, with much explanation regarding why the expectation or boundary is important in our family, and then we simply hold them accountable to it. Crazy thing is that you will likely deal with peer pressure at the same time your teens are in the throws of it.

It is not easy to look around and realize that you are the only parents who are setting up conservative boundaries and doing your absolute best to hold to them. You will begin to question whether or not you are going overboard. You wonder if your children will be scarred, and if you're just being prude. You will need to answer all of those questions in your own heart and mind before tackling these difficult topics with your children.

What motivates us? I don't want to minimize this at all. I know how hard standing your ground alone can be, and it pales in comparison to the argument you may have on your hands with your child when you try to set guidelines. So, what motivates us parents to set the guidelines we have chosen?

Well, if our biggest concern is that our children feel like they are fitting in, that they are comfortable in the groups they have chosen, or that they are dressing in the most current styles, then maybe we have a little more wiggle room in the standards being set. If our motivation is that we feel a certain conviction about their level of modesty, a conviction of the way they are representing themselves, or if we feel like our standards are about protecting their dignity and character, then I think we need to hold our ground.

Let's Ask the Lifeguards

What encouragement would you give parents of teens as they approach the issue of peer pressure?

My parents gave me too much wiggle room. Parents need to realize their kids are kids and they are the parents. We need our parents. Don't give us too much of a leash. Show your children why they should stay in the yard (within the boundaries you have set for your family). (Andrew)

You don't want to control your kids so much that they rebel, but you don't want to cut them so much slack that they go off the deep end. Every kid is different. Pray about it and talk to other parents, seek godly advice. (Jace)

In our homes (Christians), sometimes instead of directing our kids toward Christ we direct them away from things they shouldn't be a part of. I knew what was right and I knew what I wasn't supposed to do. Unless it is centered around Jesus, there is no meat in it. Focus on Jesus instead of the problem. (Andrew)

It is important for young people to find an adult with whom they can confide in and trust to walk through this with them—someone who has been in that boat. Parents often just throw out the rulebook. People that are making fun of them now will regret it one day and will have to live with those consequences. (Luke)

How did your parents do in dealing with peer pressure in your teen years?

I couldn't take them telling me what to do...not so much telling me what to do, but not hearing my side of the story. (Jace)

I thought my parents were way too involved. They wanted to know where I was going, what I was doing, and who I was with...I didn't enjoy that. (Stephanie H.)

I thought my parents were overprotective. Looking back on it now, I know they were just being parents. Every movie I wanted to see we first had to look up on Focus on the Family's Plugged In. (Andrew)

Teen years are the identity crisis capital of the world. My parents wanted me to just be me, and I wanted to be someone else. I wanted to be popular. They wanted me to hang out with people who wanted to be with me, and I wanted to hang out with people who probably didn't want to hang out with me. (Luke)

I can look back and go *man, I would do the same thing if I was a parent* on most of the things I was annoyed by...all they were doing was loving me, sometimes they might love you a little too much, but it was all done with a good heart. (Jace)

The Perfect Family? Yeah Right!

Families are as unique as snowflakes, all with their own charm, and you won't find another exactly like yours. Still, not one of them is perfect. Over 50% of marriages ending in divorce that leaves the entire family in its wake. Other struggles that families face might involve addiction, loss, sickness, financial difficulties, and just plain uncertainty. Some family struggles are visible. When loss, sickness or divorce happens, it can look like active drowning to those who are looking on from the shore. However there are other struggles that happen below the surface, like addictions or adultery. Visibility, or the lack thereof, is not a gauge of severity. Just because a family may seem "perfect" in comparison to yours doesn't mean it is. It's a mirage. We are all treading water in one way or another.

Let's ask the Lifeguards

What is it like for others to view your family as perfect?

People think our family is perfect, but they have no idea of our struggle. I process through talking and have to say what is on my mind. I am careful whom I say things to because I want to protect my family. But at the same time I can't bottle things up. There are certain people I can talk to and be totally honest with. (Christian)

It is a burden when people think your family is perfect, unless it is. And no families are perfect. It is very difficult when people think your family is perfect but you are struggling, especially when you can't talk about it. It's tough—there is a lot expected from you. Even the community expects a lot from you. (Andrew)

What do we do when others see our family as "perfect" yet we know that we have our own problems, struggles, and failures? The Lifeguards wanted to protect their families and didn't want to feel as though they were betraying the confidence of their families. However, they desired the space to be real and vulnerable. Most of the group agreed that it is a burden when people think your family is perfect. It puts a lot of pressure on your family and on you. It is very hard because no one has a perfect family. We all have days when we feel like we hit a homerun and then days when we just want to run.

Some days your kite flies high and some days it gets stuck in a tree.
Kid President

We all feel like a failure some days, and as a mom, I have felt like a failure many days. Brian and I certainly don't do everything right, and that may be the understatement of the century. We have never done everything right and neither does your family. Perfection isn't the goal anyway—the goal is loving well and being authentic.

From my experience as the Executive Director of a pregnancy center, this generation is intolerant of few things, but what they are certainly intolerant of is hypocrisy. I do not advocate sharing personal struggles in unsafe places for the dignity of your family. But when we wear masks so as to paint an image of our family having it all together with no difficulties, we teach our teens to be frauds. Our families, our children, *we* will never be perfect, and no one expects us to be. Love the Lord. Love your family. Seek first His kingdom and all other things will be taken care of.

Treading Tips

Be affectionate with your spouse. It brings security to our teens when they can trust in our relationship as husband and wife. Your marriage is an anchor to them and when the water gets choppy, can be a lighthouse on the shore.

Be affectionate with your teen. They need to feel tended to and loved, even when they are two heads taller than you.

Remember that the teenage years exist in very hostile waters. Our homes should be places of peace and refuge.

Set a time in your mind when you leave the events of your own day behind so you can fully focus on your family. I do this as I drive home from work in the afternoon, you know, putting those things behind you and pressing on.

Begin thinking of how you were affected by peer pressure as

a teen. Now, multiply that times a thousand because of social media, etc. Try to empathize with your teen, showing them compassion while still setting high standards for them.

Accept the fact that there is no such thing as the perfect child or the perfect family. It is okay to be real and face weakness. Perfection isn't the goal anyway—the goal is to love well. Our families, our children, *we* will never be perfect, and no one expects us to be. Love the Lord. Love your family. Seek first His kingdom and all other things will be taken care of.

Life Preservers

Marriage should be honored by all, and the marriage bed kept pure, for God will judge the adulterer and all the sexually immoral.

Hebrews 13:4

However, each one of you also must love his wife as he loves himself, and the wife must respect her husband.

Ephesians 5:33

Children are a heritage from the Lord, offspring a reward from him.

Psalm 127:3

But if serving the Lord seems undesirable to you, then choose for yourselves this day whom you will serve, whether the gods your ancestors served beyond the Euphrates, or the gods of the Amorites, in whose land you are living. But as for me and my household, we will serve the Lord.

Joshua 24:15

Listen, my son, to your father's instruction and do not forsake your mother's teaching.

Proverbs 1:8

Start children off on the way they should go, and even when they are old they will not turn from it.

Proverbs 22:6

Faith/Identity

Yet to all who did receive him, to those who believed in his name, he gave the right to become children of God...
John 1:12

Faith was a part of my life ever since I can remember. I loved the Lord and accepted Him as my Savior when I was five years old. My dad was diligent developing in us a love of the Bible and faithfully read us kids a Bible story before bed every night. In fact, I started reciting those stories when I was only eighteen months old. My sister, dad, and I would discuss the meaning of the scriptures and how they applied to our everyday life. My parents did a great job of giving me a firm foundation of faith and instilling the Word in my heart.

In my early teen years, a young man came to our church to speak about his journey of faith. This young man had been addicted to drugs and alcohol and had spent some time in prison due to those addictions. In prison, he ran headlong into the arms of a loving Father who saved him and set him free from his addictions. As I listened, I was so envious of the relationship with the Lord he described. I loved his story and was afraid I would never have a story of my own. I mean, after all, I had loved Him as long as I could remember. What a boring story that was destined to be!

Even at that point in my life, I felt the calling of the Lord. I wanted to serve Him. I wanted to be involved in advancing the kingdom and winning people to Christ. It was my heart's desire. As long as my faith was strong and I kept my eyes focused, not on the waves, but on the Savior who could tread on them, my identity was secure.

Don't we all wish that we could download certain life lessons directly into the hearts of our children? I know I would love to spoon-feed them their decision on drugs, sex outside of marriage, and texting while driving. I wish that I could take all of my life experience and all the moments I've shared with the Father and allow my kids to benefit from them, to nurture their spirits in the same way they did mine. I would love for them to experience the first breathe of freedom following a miraculous, yet painful season I've shared with Him. I would love for them to share in the humble gratitude I have felt after seeing a precious young woman declare Jesus her Savior for the first time. It would save so much worry and many sleepless nights if somehow all of my stumbles, my faithful moments—and my faithless ones too, my small victories, and my sobs before Him could create the same result in my children as they have created in me. The fact of the matter is that decisions become our own and we take them seriously when they cost us something. And we must arrive at the destination on our own, one step at a time.

Encouraging our teens to attend church every Sunday and go to summer camp with their youth group does not equal them having their own personal relationship with Christ. I wish that our teens having perfect attendance in Sunday school and a ribbon for the most gold stars or bringing their Bible and friends each week would somehow equal them having a sold-out, intimate relationship with the Savior. It just simply doesn't.

Now, don't get me wrong, our teens need to be involved in church. As a Christian parent, it's important to teach God's commands "to your children, talking about them when you sit at home and when you walk along the road, when you lie down and when you get up." (Deuteronomy 11:19) Much of parenting is "caught" and not "taught." The way you live your life is an example for your teen.

Encourage your teenager to have his or her own time with the Lord each day. Ask them what the Lord is teaching them. Ask them how you can pray specifically for them. Pray scripture over your teens each night before bed.

Modeling a personal relationship with Christ can encourage children to swim out alone into the deeper waters of faith in Him. The current of finding one's identity in Christ can be overwhelming. But your example could be the anchor that holds them steady in their own journey.

Let's ask the Lifeguards

As a parent I would like to know what to beware of as my teen approaches the college years. Why was it important for you to have a strong personal relationship with Christ before you sought a church home in college?

It was hard for me going off to college and having to visit and find a church on my own. If young people aren't making an effort, then maybe their faith isn't real in their own heart. If I love Jesus, I will seek out time with Him. (Christian)

I love Jesus and I follow Him, but growing up, church to me was the most boring place I ever went. I made up games to play in church to pass the time. When I was young and immature I was forced to go to church. I sat there and tried to find people with fake hair, but as I grew up, I realized I could gain from church. When I went to college it was a must for me, I had to go. When I have children, we will go to church. Know and love your kids enough to be patient with their walk. Their desire to go to church won't be the same as yours. Have Sunday centered on Jesus. (Andrew)

When I went to college everything changed, and it felt like there was no place for me in church. Churches don't have a place for college students. I feel lost when I go to some churches. (Kaylee)

I live in New York, and I go to church learn, but really they are teaching things I learned in preschool. I have a hard time going when I can watch my home church online and get a deeper message. I do think fellowship at church is important, but I really love a small men's group because we can work though issues together. That is when I go—when it isn't just a matter of being preached at, then you can't just zone out. In a discussion, you are drawn in. Iron sharpens iron. (Jace)

I prayed for girls to connect with in college and the Lord gave me that, but then I transferred to another school. I took for granted that I would have the same thing there. I was so spiritually dry. I was going to church but I wasn't being fed. It is so important to have that small group. They are encouraging, loving on you, and giving you spiritual truth. Seek those people out. (Layne)

Do teens compartmentalize their faith?

Yes, we compartmentalize. We have been taught to. On the way to church, you get in a fight and your mom is like, "Hey, zip it! We are on our way into church. Get your smiles on." So, yes: we *do* compartmentalize, and it is hard to fight that. (Christian)

I feel like it is kinda easy to do that. But for me, sitting in that pew I feel so convicted. Here I am worshipping God, but where was I twelve hours ago? I will be honest, I have sat in church hungover. It is easy to do, but it is hard because you feel so guilty. (Tate)

We have all felt the emptiness of getting caught up in life. Naturally, our attention is drawn so many directions, and even if it isn't wrong, it takes our focus from Him. I don't know if I am Mary or Martha; I am a little Mary-Martha. It is so easy to get caught up doing life and forget to be still before God, especially when you are forced to you feel convicted—like, am I doing this for everyone else here? (Andrew)

When THE Lion speaks a Word over you...

Entering high school, I had a pretty good grasp of the Word. I was involved in my youth group at church, but the intimacy of my relationship with the Lord waned. Even though I had a good group of friends, when my identity became about what others thought of me, I completely imploded.

I became consumed with what other people thought of me. Was I popular? Did I have a lot of friends? Did I have *any* friends? Did I have any *real* friends? I had many of the same thoughts that young people have today.

As high school began, so did my attempt to create myself a story. I began to make many compromises and concessions. I could relate to Paul because I did the things I knew I shouldn't and didn't do the things I knew I should. I violated truths that I knew were Biblically founded. I participated in activities that I knew went not only against my faith, but against my family—against everything that I had been raised to believe. By my choosing, I experienced a fairly intense season of rebellion, and it lead to many consequences that I would live out over the course of my lifetime.

After high school, I found myself going to a community college and really didn't know what I wanted to do. I was struggling with identity and was grasping at anything that might help me get on track. I decided I would have more opportunity if I moved to Dallas, Texas, a large metroplex not too far from home. I applied to be a flight attendant with a large airline and went pretty deep into the interview process. My mom and my grandmother traveled with me to Dallas for one of the interviews. That afternoon, we went to the movies (this will certainly date me). We saw Disney's *The Lion King*. You will get a better grasp of the depths of this statement later in the book, but I had put my family through a lot at this point. I had broken their hearts. I was trying to recommit to the Lord and to find my way, but in the not-so-distant past I had really wounded my family, and I was very ashamed of the things I had done. That little girl who could quote Bible verses and who felt called to serve somehow in ministry seemed like a long time passed.

Isn't it so like the Father to use unexpected moments to reach us? One of the most profound moments in my faith walk was in that Dallas movie theater. There is a scene in *The Lion King* where Simba, feeling responsible for his father's death, runs from his calling and destiny out of fear and shame. Simba is living a life contrary to his calling and neglecting his inheritance. At one point in the movie, he has a vision of his dad, Mufasa. Mufasa tells him, "Remember who you are."

I was struck by those words. I was at a place in life that I needed to remember who the Lord said I was—who did *He* say that I was? Maybe you, too, haven't lived every moment in a way that is honoring of your inheritance. Maybe you look nothing like the person that God called, ordained, prepared, and equipped you to be; maybe your teenager doesn't either...yet, the callings of the Lord are irrevocable. (Romans 11:29) When He speaks a word over you, He does not take it back.

This was a pivotal moment in my faith journey, because I began to passionately pursue Him and the callings that little girl had held in her heart. I revisited all of those Bible stories that I had loved and began to return to my first Love. I realized when I was a young child my identity was in Him. The rebellion I experienced in my teen years was due to allowing my identity to be caught up in other people rather than in Him.

Teaching your teen to find value and identity in the Lord is more critical than teaching them to eat healthy and helping them get into the university of their choice. Remind your teenager of the Lord's calling on their life. Recall with them memories of when the Lord used them in someone else's life or gave them divine direction or favor. Use specific events in their life to validate that they are truly who God says they are and that He has good plans for them.

Our Lifeguard, Jace, is a wrestler and a phenomenal one, I might add. I met Jace at a wrestling tournament when he was about thirteen years old, and he impressed me even then. Jace comes from a strong Christian family. He was home schooled until high school and then attended a public school to be a part of the wrestling team.

When Jace started high school he didn't really know anyone, and he will joke that, for almost all of his freshman year, the kids called him "backpack boy." But it didn't take long for people to start taking note of his wrestling ability. He is very focused on his sport and very committed. Pretty soon, all of his peers and many adults associated him with wrestling.

Jace began to feel like his identity was in his wrestling success. His identity became wrestling. If he won a match or a tournament, he felt good about himself and he felt like others were proud of him. If he lost, however, he felt like a failure and believed the love and approval from others was related to his performance on the mat.

During his sophomore year of high school, Jace wrestled in the state finals match and came up short with a second place finish. He hit the bottom. He felt like a failure and a disappointment. He was sinking in the violent waves of an identity crisis.

Jace recalls attending a Wednesday night service where his youth pastor began to talk about identity. The pastor said, "If your identity is in your academic success, your musical ability, your popularity, or in a sport that you participate in, then you are on shaky ground. Your identity is found in Christ alone."

That was a life preserver moment for Jace. He will describe it as a turning point. It was in that moment when he realized his athletic ability was a tool God had given him to gain glory for Himself and a tool for Jace to point people back to Him. Jace began to wrestle only to glorify His Father. That changed everything.

Until his shift in perspective, I had heard Jace frequently refer to himself as, "The King of Second Place." After dumping that false title, his wrestling improved and he gained inner strength as well. Jace became a state champion in high school and is now on the wrestling team at Cornell University. He is victorious on the mat, but he is a champion because his identity is in Christ alone.

Let's ask the Lifeguards

What can parents do if they have a teenager who is struggling with their faith?

You have to know why you believe what you believe. You shouldn't believe just because your parents do. I believe in absolute truth and that if you seek it, you will find it. Of course there is absolute truth. All religions can be wrong, but only one could possibly be right. Every founder of every other religion gets money, power, or sex. They all get something out of it for themselves except for Christianity. What did Jesus get? He was beaten and crucified, and not one fact in the Bible can be disproven. It takes more faith to be an atheist. Parents, if you have a teen questioning, if they are seeking truth and listening for the Lord, don't even worry about them. He will speak to them, bet the farm on it. I base my life on it. (Jace)

My parents were missionaries and I still questioned. I am proud of that because I know what I believe and why I believe for myself, not because of my parents. (Kaylee)

I was saved very young, at six years old. All of my childhood, people would say you need to be sure that you know that you know that you know. One night I asked my mom, "do you think that I am really saved and does the Lord live in my heart?" My mom said, "yes, I know He does," and she reminded me of specific things in my life that testified to the fact that the Lord was living in me. (Layne)

What does your generation need from mine for you to be authentic in your faith?

I need the bar set higher. Right now, it's if you don't have sex and you go to church then that's good enough and well, there you go. The expectations are so low that you can almost skirt around it, make your parents happy but still do what you want. I would have loved to have a bar set through the sky. That is what I would have loved. (Jace)

We need a higher mark we are aiming for. We need your generation to believe we can do it. There are so many people who talk to us like we have already failed. I have great hope in our generation. We are taking on difficult issues. I don't think we are a failure. It is our turn to take it over, but we are talked down to a lot. We need encouragement and we need the bar set real high. That isn't going to make us think, *oh that is too high we can't do that.* It will push us and encourage us to be better. (Christian)

People look down on us. People who know me know the type of man I am; they know me, and they expect certain things of me. We need our parents to raise us, not society, especially how our world is now. I am talking YOU: raise your child. There isn't a perfect family dynamic, but if you want certain values in your kids, you have to be the ones to raise them. It isn't easy, but instill life and hope in them. (Andrew)

While all the issues that we've discussed about faith and identity are important, there is no decision more important than the decision to be a Christ follower. What do we as parents do if we have a child that is wrestling with their own decision about what they will do with the Savior? I have listened to many scared and emotional parents describe one of their children experiencing a spiritual identity crisis. I've not heard more heart-felt pain than a parent literally crying out over their child's eternity.

Remember the story in Genesis 32, when Jacob wrestles with the

Lord? There are a few things I would like to point out:

1. Just a chapter before, Jacob makes a covenant with his father-in-law, Laban, and in verse 53, Jacob takes the oath in the name of the *Fear of his father Isaac* (italics are mine). In Genesis 32:9, Jacob is praying to the Lord. He is preparing to see his brother Esau for the first time since Jacob stole Esau's blessing. Jacob is afraid, to say the least. He sends bribes ahead hoping to pacify Esau, but he is keenly aware that Esau is coming to meet him and he is bringing over 400 men along. In Jacob's prayer, he refers to the Lord as *O God of my Father Abraham, God of my father Isaac, O Lord*...Do you notice that Jacob views God as the God of his fathers, but he doesn't make reference to Him being *his* God?

2. In chapter 32, the Word tells us that Jacob wrestled with God all night, and when morning was coming, the Lord tells him to let Him go. Jacob replies, "I will not let you go unless you bless me." (Genesis 32:26). The Lord asks Jacob, "What is your name?" Strange question isn't it? Why in the world would He ask him his name at a moment like this? Because as soon as Jacob utters his name, he is confessing himself a "deceiver"...taking responsibility for his past and confessing it to the Lord.

3. Finally, the Lord changes Jacob's name from "deceiver" to "Israel"—him who struggles with God. Israel called the place of their struggle Peniel, which means, "It is because I saw God face to face, and yet my life was spared."

4. This experience changed Jacob's gate for the rest of his life. He walked with a limp from that moment forward.

Those of us who have a child or someone we love experiencing a spiritual identity crisis can gain much comfort and encouragement from this story. Jacob was a grandson of father Abraham. His father, Isaac, laid himself on an altar to be sacrificed because of his faith and that of his father Abraham. Yet, Jacob had to have his own wrestling match with the Lord. Jacob had to take ownership for his own past and shortcomings and wrestle the thing through with the Lord. And then...he called the Lord *his* God and knew that he had seen God face to face for himself.

The same is true for our children. They must put their own hand to the question, asking themselves what to do with this man they call Jesus. They will own up to their own past and shortcomings and there will certainly be painful moments, life-changing moments. But when all is said and done, they will have seen Him face to face, and He will have changed their gate, and their walk with Him will never be the same. We can trust them to the process; our God hasn't lost a wrestling match yet.

Treading Tips

A lack of identity is prevalent due in part to the influence social media. Selfies are pictures people take of themselves and then post on some form of social media, whether that's Facebook, Twitter, Instagram, or any of the other multitudes of options available to them. Often times, when someone posts a selfie, it's to get a response. We have many examples of young women asking, "Do you think I'm beautiful?" or "How would you rate me?" How dangerous to rely on a number of votes on a selfie to establish value. It's just not healthy. If you have a young person regularly participating in this type of activity, we should be asking ourselves, *what is it that they are asking their peers for?*—their peers who simply do not have the capacity to give them what they need.

Pray scripture over your teen at night. Encourage them in their own personal relationship with Christ.

When we see our teenagers compromising their values we need to dig deeper to determine if there is an identity issue. Drinking, going too far physically in a dating relationship, hanging around people who they would have never hung out with before; making compromises in the things they have stood for…all of these are red flags.

If your teen refuses to participate in family Bible study or refuses to attend church, they could be struggling with identity. I don't believe this is uncommon, and you shouldn't freak-out or panic if you have to drag your teen out of bed on Sunday mornings; however, maintain your position. Our family attends church; our family participates in Bible study. Encourage your kids to continue to participate because the Word does not return void (Isaiah 55:11). This is especially important difficult times, when they may be struggling with their identity, the Word will build us up and remind us of who He says we are.

Our children aren't singers, musicians, scholars, athletes, punks, prudes, etc. They may be good at those things, but they shouldn't identify themselves with a single hobby, talent, or interest. They are beloved children of the King who may be gifted at or talented in many different things. Remind them of their calling. Validate the things they have seen God do in their own lives.

If your child begins to ask questions regarding faith, don't allow fear to slip in. Trust the Father through the process. He's a master swimmer. Heck, He doesn't even need to swim. He can just reach down and take them for a stroll on the waves.

Set the bar high. Great expectations give our teens something to strive for. Low expectations can be hurtful to teens and harm their self-esteem. There is value and fulfillment in working hard to achieve greatness. Encourage your teen to aim high!

Remember, God hasn't lost a wrestling match yet: He is faithful to His promises.

Life Preservers

So God created mankind in his own image, in the image of God he created them; male and female he created them.

Genesis 1:27

Therefore, if anyone is in Christ, the new creation has come: The old has gone, the new is here!

2 Corinthians 5:17

But you are a chosen people, a royal priesthood, a holy nation, God's special possession, that you may declare the praises of him who called you out of darkness into his wonderful light.

1Peter 2:9

You were taught, with regard to your former way of life, to put off your old self, which is being corrupted by its deceitful desires; to be made new in the attitude of your minds; and to put on the new self, created to be like God in true righteousness and holiness.

Ephesians 4:22-24

I have been crucified with Christ and I no longer live, but Christ lives in me. The life I now live in the body, I live by faith in the Son of God, who loved me and gave himself for me.

Galatians 2:20

Teens, Sex, and Society

Sometimes it's hard to tell how fast the current's moving until you're headed over a waterfall.
Kimberly McCreight

Overwhelming. The way that our culture has perverted sexuality can just be flat overwhelming. Keeping up with all of our teens' events along with their math grades can be a full time job. I completely understand that trying to stay on top of all of the latest terms and issues surrounding teen sexuality can put us right over the edge. Because their science test and speech for student council seems more urgent, we often put off educating ourselves on uncomfortable societal topics until tomorrow. Due to the consequences related to teens having sex outside of marriage, and to the fact that some of those consequences can be lifelong, we can put it off no longer. Today is the new tomorrow.

Something that amazed me throughout my time with the Lifeguards was that many of the things society tells us about the way teens think and the things they desire from their parents didn't seem to be the case, at least not with this group. We can see this from their advice: don't give your kids too much wiggle room, set boundaries and explain to your teens why it is important to stay within them, and date in groups (don't do the one-on-one thing). These tips from the Lifeguards, and many others like them, are the very stances that can keep us up at night worried our teens may hate us and will be out the door at their first opportunity. The truth is, at least from our Lifeguards' perspectives, that our teenagers need us to take the stand that we feel the Lord has called us to take as their parents even if, at the time, they push back against it.

Who doesn't love the idea of a beautiful love story penned by the romantic of all eternity? God is love. He understands it; He relates to us through it; He embodies it. He stepped into this concept of "time" with us so that we could walk with Him in the cool of the garden, but also on the stormy waves of the sea...because of Love. He loves us. He desires intimacy. He gave His son for our salvation, but also to destroy the veil, the divide that was between us, so that we could each have our own intimate relationship with Him.

Our God is the designer of sex. It is not good for man to be alone. Every human being has the desire to be seen, understood, and loved. We crave to be intimately connected to another while being completely vulnerable and exposed. Isn't that the purpose of sex? And it is a covenant, a promise between husband and wife, sealed in blood, as are all covenants. God is the creator and author of love and intimacy.

Is it any wonder that the enemy would launch a full-on attack on love and sexuality, one of the most intimate acts humans participate in (the most intimate except for worship, in my opinion). Why would the enemy care to attack sexuality and marital love? Because he gives two hoots and a holler about our happiness or lack thereof? Absolutely not. He wants to break the heart of the Father, and you and I and our children happen to be the closest things to His heart.

The thief comes only to steal and kill and destroy...

John 10:10

The enemy loves to steal from our children the innocence and beauty of sex shared only between husband and wife. He loves to kill the dream of a beautiful love story penned by the Author specifically for them. This battlefield has the potential to kill, in the literal sense, through sexually transmitted diseases and to break hearts over a sinful, empty approach to sexuality.

The enemy loves to destroy trust in relationships between husband and wife over infidelity or pornography. He loves to destroy trust between you and your teenager. Most importantly, the enemy loves to destroy our teens' image of God, by painting Him as a prude killjoy. When, all the while, God orchestrated sex to bless and fulfill.

...I have come that they may have life, and have it to the full.
John 10:10

It is our enemy who uses sex to destroy.

Everywhere our children go and everything they see, from TV commercials to magazines at the checkout aisle in the grocery line, not to mention technology, they are bombarded with sexual images. They are inundated with other people's opinions about sex.

God is the Creator, the only being who can make something beautiful and complete from literally nothing, using only His Word. He created sex to foster intimacy and bonding between a husband, a wife, and Himself. God designed sex to be beautiful and beneficial in a committed, lifelong, marital relationship. But sex is a lot like fire. If we obey the rules associated with fire, if we use fire the way it is designed, it is a blessing. But if we refuse to follower the Designer's instructions for sex, the same as with fire, it can be all consuming and devastating. Those who play with fire or sex will find themselves bearing permanent scars.

As with all of the topics we discuss in this book, we must ask ourselves if these standards are achievable. Do you believe that our goal can be for our children, boys and girls, to maintain sexual integrity? It is imperative that we first answer that question in our own heart.

Let's Ask the Lifeguards

What are your thoughts on the constant peer pressure teens face to be sexually active?

 It was easier for me once someone explained *why* I shouldn't

have sex—what God says about sex and why it can be harmful outside of marriage. (Christian)

In middle school and high school, you may struggle with your identity while others are experimenting, but in college it's different...me choosing to save sex for marriage on a football team. The first couple months of college I was made fun of so much, and it got old after a while. But after that, it was like testing to see if I was legit. So many Christians are fake nowadays—they were testing to see if I was who I said I was, and when I stood through that, there was a higher level of respect than I could have ever gotten by sleeping with a lot of girls. I was then looked at as a leader. (Andrew)

You do things just to fit in, maybe even things you know are wrong...just to feel wanted by people. (Stephanie P.)

Recently, I was having a conversation with women that I looked up to in a lot of ways and we got on the topic of the ring on my finger to signify that I am saving myself for marriage, and they made comments that let me know this was foreign to them...and these were people I had really looked up to. It is hard to realize that it is almost a joke now. I was almost laughed at. I was laughed at. (Layne)

I still to this day get ragged on hard by all my buddies. At this point they just make a joke out of it. The more times you make that decision (to abstain), though, the temptation is hardly there. That has been the most important thing for me making that decision over and over. It becomes a habit. (Jace)

As a parent, I know the topic of sexuality pierces straight to our hearts. Few temptations that our children will face are as powerful and frequent as this. Sexuality is a dichotomy: it has the power to destroy; yet, in the fullness of time and under the cover of the covenant of marriage and the blessing of the Father, it brings life, intimacy, and blessing. Remember, parenting is an act of worship on our part. We simply seek Him and then with quiet resolve and peace, we turn to these gifts the Father entrusted to us and point them in the way they should go without fear, without dread, but full of hope in all of the good plans that lay ahead.

I am privileged to speak to parents on a regular basis, and when the topic of discussing sex with our teens comes up, a hush falls over the crowd. When I am speaking with parents and I tell them most experts believe you should talk to your children about sex by age eight, you can almost cut the tension with a knife.

Parents are fearful and simply do not want to rob children of innocence or expose them to these kinds of discussions before it is absolutely necessary. However, if you have waited until your child is a teen to talk about sexual purity, you are too late. Maintaining good communication with our children is so important to maintaining a healthy connection. When we can speak openly with them about all things, like we discussed in the chapter on communication, it makes it much easier to cover the more difficult issues, like sex.

Most of us grew up during the time of the "one time" talk or no talk at all. I did have the talk, if you can call it that, from my mother and my grandmother. I came home from school one day in the seventh grade and found my mom and my grandmother sitting on the couch looking at me with their best June Cleaver smiles. My mom said, "We bought you a book and left it on your bed. Would you go and read through it? If you have any questions come and ask us."

I went to my room and discovered the book, *The Wonderful Way Babies are Made*. On the cover there was a goofy looking drawing of a family—they looked too happy, surely they didn't know what was within the pages of this book. No one's denying sex is wonderful and all, but to a thirteen-year-old girl, it's a bit of a test on the gag reflex. I flipped the pages as quickly as possible, opened my bedroom door, and hollered, "No questions! I think I've got it!"

I didn't want to look at my mother or grandmother after that, much less talk to them, and I am certain they felt the same way. Those "sex talk" moments are always awkward—to hear your parents saying those things and to imagine them doing those things can be almost more than a girl can handle! I know that my mom and grandmother were so completely relieved and thankful to put the check in that box. Because in their minds, they had covered the topic of sex once and for all; however, this approach (to hand a thirteen-year-old a book and tell them to ask questions) didn't work well back then, and it certainly doesn't now.

One of the lifeguards, Christian, told us that her dad was a doctor, so the topic of sex was never taboo. However, she did tell us that he often needed to talk to his younger patients about sex in his office because their parents didn't want to or because he was faced with so many of his teen patients becoming pregnant. But Christian tells us that the best sex education came from her youth pastor laying out the reasons why sex outside of marriage is potentially harmful.

I agree wholeheartedly that parents and adult mentors should share with young people the consequences associated with sex outside of marriage, but the fear of a pregnancy or sexually transmitted diseases are not enough to enable teens to maintain sexual purity until marriage. The shame of an unplanned pregnancy and the fear of sexually transmitted diseases aren't enough to encourage teenagers to change a negative behavior or maintain a positive one.

In John 8, we read about a woman who was caught in adultery and whom the teachers of the law and the Pharisees brought to Jesus. Undoubtedly, this woman had experienced shame over and over again (it comes with the lifestyle). She likely was talked about around the village and snickered at in the streets. She probably promised herself, out of shame and self-loathing, that she *would* change, that she *must* change. But neither the shame nor the self-loathing was strong enough motivation to provoke true change. It was the love of Christ that changed her. "Go and sin and no more." It is His beautiful love that changes us all.

Our approach to sexuality as a culture has been mediocre at best. We have hoped that if we could get all the youth to the civic center in our community and hire the right speaker to say the right things in the right way, then the light bulb would come on and our youth would say, "OH! Well, now I understand perfectly and will no longer have sex out of wedlock or behave in any other immoral way. We are all good."

It will not happen. Morality, righteousness, and holiness are taught in our homes day in and day out through the life-changing love of Christ. While general comments from other respected adults on sexual purity are important, the work of preparing your teen to walk that out is yours. Having on-going conversations about boundaries, thought life, compromising situations, and purity are vital.

Let's Ask the Lifeguards

What should parents of teens consider when talking to their teens about purity?

Be sure and tell your children why purity and postponing sex and activities leading up to sex is important. Take sexting as an example: I can tell you, as a guy, when a guy gets a picture of a girl, he shows it to every other guy there. And do you know what it does to that girl's value in the minds of all those guys? Downhill...with one little thing. (Jace)

Be a part of your children's lives and monitor them. We choose how we raise our children, and then they make their own choices. (Andrew)

We feel more safe and secure when we know and understand

the expectations and the rules. (Christian)

Rules, even those regarding dating and sex, are easier to abide by if there is a healthy, strong relationship with your parents. (Stefanie P)

If you have a good relationship, then they trust you and they are willing to obey you. If they have a goal to remain sexually pure, your job as a parent is to help them get there. It gives them purpose. (Jace)

If parents are fighting our battles, then when we face a battle we will phone a friend every time. Let us fight our own battles. There are times that parents need to step in, but mostly let them struggle through it. Give them (teens) tools, advice, and encouragement, but raise a man—raise a woman. (Andrew)

How can parents help their kids in their desire to be sexually pure?

In my journey to keep myself pure, my dad is the most important person. The biggest way he has helped me is from a young age he has been telling me I am beautiful, adequate, and capable. He isn't just saying those things. He really believes them. I believe them now because he has said them so many times. Tell your teens who they are. We don't know who we are. We are trying to figure that out. We need someone to tell us. Dads are so important for girls. (Christian)

Moms don't usually tell their sons, "Hey, be pure." I needed that from my mom. I had no idea how girls are. I have a sister, but my brother and I picked on her so much that she's a tomboy...I don't know how girls act or that they are manipulating me. I mean,

I got played by girls a few times because I had no idea. Girls are bad at that. You need to listen to your mom when she says, "Hey, I don't think she's a good one." Even my dad sometimes still doesn't see it. Your mom needs to be a part. (Jace)

I know a lot of dads who treat their daughters incredible, and yet their daughters still make mistakes, and a lot of the time I don't think it's the parents' complete fault. There's a lot of stuff you just can't protect your kids from. The way you deal with that is the kids have to make their own decisions. So you need to teach them why you have set the boundaries you have, you've got to show them the benefits and explain the problems. They make their own decision, and then this isn't just a rule, it is a lifestyle. (Jace)

In the moment, it isn't enough for our parents to have told us not to; we have to know why (why the teen is choosing sexual purity for themselves). (Christian)

I didn't grow up with a good father, so really my purity is all about my relationship with God. I know that God says I am a princess and that's what I have to stand firm on. (Stefanie P.)

I talk to both my parents about the differences in men and women. You have to connect and relate to people. Parents need to relate to their kids and be honest. Parents are afraid their kids will see them differently and kids are afraid to be honest with their parents about their struggles for fear we will see them differently. We both need to be open and transparent. (Andrew)

If you were the parent of a teenager, what would you say to them about purity and dating?

Girls, I've got something else to say. If you are the one pursuing the guy, then why do you expect him to be the leader later? Let him pursue you. Guys want to be the one pursuing. When the time comes, let the guy pursue you. Prince Charming still has a high voice at age fourteen. Give him time to grow up, be patient. (Andrew)

You can tell those guys who stay true to themselves. Girls notice guys that stand up for what they believe in, and if you stay true to that, God has a great person for you. (Layne)

You need to be thankful for the veil the Lord has put over you and that is on purpose. He is protecting you. Don't try to rip that off and say *no, I want this now*. Be thankful for the protection. It is a good thing. (Christian)

Girls want to take care of and help. Women see a guy with potential and they want to fix them. You can't fix anyone. A lot of girls seek a change in someone, and when they don't change, they claim all guys are the same. If you know that going in, you can't be surprised when they don't change. (Andrew)

It is definitely a struggle to stay pure in this fallen world. I feel like these days you are an outcast if you are a virgin, because it is so uncommon. (Stephanie H.)

I think it is important to teach children about what sex should really be about. It is not something to be thrown about freely, but rather a gift from the Lord to be cherished. (Theresa)

It is dangerous to start having physical relationships as a teen, because it puts teens in situations they are not ready for emotionally, socially, or physically. (Layne)

✍ The real temptation starts at puberty. All of a sudden the testosterone starts cooking and all of a sudden girls look way different than they did a minute ago and by that time they are a little more mature than you are. That's when I started getting tempted. (Jace)

✍ Pray. I was covered in prayer, and I continually prayed about it (maintaining my purity). (Layne)

✍ Obviously they (your peers) will call you a homosexual right off the bat (once your peers realize you are abstaining from sex) and say you can't get girls. They say you don't because you can't get girls, which causes another issue because you get insecure about it and, okay, so you don't do sex, but you start going down this road a little bit because you want to prove to all your friends that you *can* get girls. If I were going to help a kid, I would tell him the benefits of not doing it. A lot of people don't see the huge benefits of not doing that. We need to share that with kids to help them. People come to me with problems because I don't have sex. It is the ultimate witnessing tool, because people can't fathom that, as a twenty-two-year-old, I am still a virgin. (Jace)

✍ Scripture is our only offensive weapon. If I were talking to someone trying to stay pure, I would tell them the benefits of waiting, who they are in Christ, and then how to fight it with scripture and the Word. (Andrew)

✍ Accountability is huge. Where you left off with the last guy is where you start off with the next. (Stephanie H.)

Make sure you are on the same page with a person you are dating. Be specific about deep things. Be detailed about where you are setting the bar. (Layne)

Modesty, Dating, and Sexting

I would like to spend some time talking about the temptations that our teens face growing up in this culture. I am a bystander on a beachfront...I have seen many teenagers try to swim out in some pretty high seas. I have seen some of them bitten by the more stealthy enemies who thrive in the chaos of the current. I have seen some of them taken down by very large squalls that can take out dozens of unsuspecting teens at once. And I have seen a few hang a perfect ten as they literally surf right over the top of it.

I feel like it is the Lord's desire for all of us, especially parents, to simply say to those heading into the water, "Hey, not trying to butt in or steal your fun, but it seems to work best for the guys who..." or "You know, I've not yet seen a young man successfully swim straight into that twenty-foot wave and make it out unscathed."

Dating

Many families allow their thirteen and fourteen year olds to date by dropping them off at the movies, letting them to watch movies at one another's homes, texting and talking on the phone, and going to school dances together. Statistically, if young people start "dating" in the sixth grade (which is very common), then 91% of the time they will have sex before graduating high school. Sex is progressive. If we allow the progression to begin too young, we are simply fighting a losing battle. It is far easier to delay dating and similar activities than it is to allow it and then try to pull back the boundary. Be thoughtful about beginning the progression of a teen's dating relationship and seek the Lord before you permit it to start. Once you do, they have jumped on a surf board and are paddling out into the waves. Make sure they know the rules of swimming in such aggressive waters.

Bikinis/inappropriate dress

I am not and do not want to ever be the morality police. I don't think that I have the ability or authority to set guidelines for other families on what is appropriate and inappropriate dress or anything else for that matter. But please understand that people do make assumptions about us and our children based on our appearances. When we allow our daughters to wear immodest clothing, people, including young men, are not thinking about what a bright, darling young lady she is. Sure, a young man notices bodies in immodest swimming suits, but all that our daughters will have earned are a few moments of attention. The search for true beauty continues, and we have given our daughters the wrong message about what that beauty really is.

Sexting

In January of 2014, the Journal of Pediatric Medicine reported that 1 in 5 middle school (pre-teens and teens) children have engaged in sexting. Though the frequency of sexting shows little gender variation, the pressure to participate in sexting is considerably stronger for girls. Fifty-one percent of teen girls said pressure from a guy was the reason they sexted, compared to just 18% of teen boys who said they felt pressure from a girl, according to a 2008 study by National Campaign to Prevent Teen and Unplanned Pregnancy and CosmoGirl.com.

A 2010 nationwide survey sponsored by LG Mobile Phones found that one-in-three teens have participated in sexting and one-in-four thinks it's a normal part of teen life. The survey also found that "for many teens, sending, receiving and forwarding these types of messages and images – and even being the target of such messages – is indicative of a higher social status."

As the Executive Director of a pregnancy center, and from

dealing with teens in mentor relationships on a very regular basis, I believe that sexting—defined as sexual language sent via text message—is common among teen boys and girls, but sending nude pictures is far more common for young ladies.

Recently I had a long visit with two different mothers. The first is the mom of a handsome, athletic, obedient, and good young man. The afternoon that she called, I could hear the pain and fear in her voice. (Situations like this are always most devastating when they seem to blind-side us.) While her son does well in school, has pretty good friendships, and spends little time alone and most of his time with his family, this heartbroken mom had just learned that he was texting one of his male friends very descriptive accounts of what he and his girlfriend had been doing sexually. True or not, if these text messages were spread through the school (and in most cases they are), this young lady's reputation would be ruined and the young man's damaged as well.

The second woman I spoke with is the mother of a beautiful, intelligent young lady who has been communicating with a young man whom her parents have forbidden her to interact with. This mother was devastated to learn that her daughter had sent multiple nude or almost nude photos of herself to this young man at his request. The young man would say things in via text like, "If you don't send me a picture, I'm not going to talk to you tomorrow," or, "If you don't send another pic, I will find someone else who will."

What these young people don't understand is that their behavior now can cause a ripple effect in their lives later on. First of all, if a girl will send nude pictures of herself to one guy, he shouldn't be so naïve to think that she wouldn't send them to other guys. Likewise, a young lady is crazy to believe that a boy who asked for nude pictures from his girlfriend won't forward these same nude pictures to his buddies and show them around the locker room. This kind of boy cannot be trusted. The sad truth is these kinds of incidents can be life altering—I have known of families forced to move away because of their children's sexting scandals. Even worse, there have been cases of suicide related to a "leak" of this sort that teens can't get over.

As a parent concerned about the well-being of your teenager, you simply must invade their privacy. Checking text messages, looking at your cell phone bill to see if there are unknown numbers, and installing applications and programs to help you monitor are so important. You simply *must* know what is going on in their world.

Pornography

Pornography is likely the enemy's strongest tool against young men. I think it can make things easier for us to imagine the enemy as an evil idiot. However, he is not. He has been on the scene since the beginning, and he has the jump on us. He has studied mankind for thousands of years and knows things that commonly trip us up.

Certainly it isn't isolated to males, but pornography is an effective trap of men. One of the young men in our lifeguards group said that this is such a common issue that he believes every man will struggle with pornography at some point. If *every* young man struggles with pornography, can we win? Or should we just through in the towel?

Pornography is a lie. It is traumatic and painful, whether or not our teens realize it to the people participating in the industry. I had the privilege to participate in a sermon series with Craig Gross from XXX Church. XXX Church ministers to women who would like to come out of the porn industry. Pornography is a lie in that sex in marriage is different. It is something beautiful. It isn't just a physical act; it is an intimate interaction physically, emotionally, and spiritually. Pornography destroys relationships on so many levels. If a young man in his teens succumbs to the trap of pornography, it can become something that continues to affect him for years to come.

Sexual temptation is so powerful that your commitment to Jesus is

the only thing strong enough to help you maintain purity.

- 93% of boys and 62% of girls are exposed to Internet porn before the age of 18.[3]
- 70% of boys have sent more than 30 consecutive minutes looking at porn on at least one occasion.
- 35% have done this on more than 10 occasions.
- 69% of boys and 55% of girls have seen porn showing same-sex intercourse.
- Only 3% of boys and 17% of girls have never seen internet pornography.[4]

Let's Ask the Lifeguards

How can parents deal with the issue of pornography with our teens?

This is a touchy subject and sometimes shameful. God says, "Among you there must not be a hint of immorality." People think pornography and they think XXX. It starts at a much smaller level. What do you allow yourself to look at or think about a woman? It doesn't start with porn; it starts much smaller.

An issue that every young man pretty much deals with is masturbation. It is almost expected. In the Bible, it never says don't do that, but it does say among you there must be no sexually immorality. The first time I did that, I was thirteen and I had no idea what I was doing. I tried to perfect masturbation so that I wasn't thinking bad thoughts. But that is almost impossible. Almost every guy you talk to will admit they have done this and it becomes an addiction. It changes how we see women and ourselves. It is something we get caught up in and it is accepted.

When I have a son, I will talk to him, but I will also let him know how I struggled with it. Scripture memory is huge in fighting your flesh. When I am tempted, I speak His words and not my own. My dad carved a niche on his computer, and every time he gets on the computer he rubs it to remind himself of his commitment. The battle continues and we have to be on guard. Stop masturbation and porn before it becomes a habit. It is hard to stop once it starts. (Andrew)

I have lot of friends who feel so horrible about it that it affects their relationship with the Lord because they feel so guilty about it. I feel horrible for a lot of men because it puts them in complete bondage. It is straight up a decision to stop that. You have to keep making the decision until it becomes a habit. If you get that feeling, read your Bible. I have done that and it helps. Or I think about my future wife...if she were watching me, what would she do? First of all, put blocks on things—on your phone, your computer, and your iPad. You need accountability partners. Try to find a friend who will make a commitment with you, and knowing someone else is depending on you will help you stop. (Jace)

I will speak up for girls. I know there are more women who have dealt with this, but you do feel alone. It isn't just a guy's struggle. It isn't something you are proud of, and you want to hide it. Certainly you rely on scripture and not on yourself. I need to give it to the Lord and know that together we will get through it. You also have to know yourself. What does tempt you? Don't be alone. If reading or running takes your mind off it, do something that. Know yourself and don't put yourself in that situation. (Layne)

When I fell to this (pornography) it wasn't about sexuality. It was usually that I felt alone. Our enemy uses a lot of things that aren't sin to lead us to it (sins, like viewing pornography). We've got to be smart (to the schemes of the enemy). (Andrew)

I asked the young men in the Lifeguards what we as parents

needed to do differently to have an effect on this issue. The comment that most stuck out to me came from Andrew:

> We need honest, transparent fathers that can be open about their own personal struggles and how they overcame them. I think young boys can handle the struggle. But it is important for them not to see their Christian dads as perfect, like Jesus, but realize that they struggled just like we do; and if they can overcome their struggles, so can we.

This is for certain, we have to discuss the hard issues with our children, be open about our own struggles, and encourage our children to struggle well. The Lifeguards also said that memorizing scripture and being disciplined to quote scripture to themselves when they felt tempted in the area of pornography was most important. The Word is our sword, our only offensive weapon in this battle we are fighting. Wield it.

Another important tip the Lifeguards gave us was to encourage our teens to not be alone when feeling tempted in this area. They need to come out of the room, go for a jog, go throw the football with their friends—anything to take their minds off of the temptation. In this world there will be trouble, but as 1 John 3:8 says, "The reason the Son of God appeared was to destroy the devil's work." Let's help our young men and women fight the battle before them for their purity.

True Beauty

There are many things I think are simply an ingrained part of the human experience, and two of them are a desire to behold true beauty and the desire to search for true beauty.

Though we travel the world over to find the beautiful, we must carry it with us or we find it not.
Ralph Waldo Emerson

The best and most beautiful things in the world cannot be seen or even touched – they are felt with the heart.
Helen Keller

Beauty is something that our daughters carry with them. It is in what they say, how they act, and how they love. It is displayed in the way they represent themselves as a daughter of the King. Beauty is who they are. Beauty is something to be protected and is valuable enough to be sought. Not to be freely handed out to anyone who happens by, beauty is something that is revealed over time and through conversations.

Beauty is something our sons seek. Searching for it only increases its value and makes it precious. Sure, they might also notice a girl's physical appearance, but deep down they know beauty is more than attractiveness.

My heart for my own teenage daughter is to realize that, as Cinderella's fairy Godmother said, "even miracles take time". I want her to know that beauty is something she is and that it will take her husband his whole life to uncover each aspect of that beauty. I want her to know that beauty is carried in the way she speaks to people, the way she makes eye contact, her ability to see others for who they really are, the way she pursues her heavenly Father, and the way she dresses and presents herself.

She warned him not to be deceived by appearances for beauty is found within.
Beauty and the Beast

I want my teenage son to know that beauty is worth the time it takes to discover the real thing. As Marie Stopes puts it, "You can take no credit for being beautiful at sixteen, but if you are beautiful at sixty, it will be your souls own doing." I want him to know that the King has a beautiful bride chosen for him and her beauty will come from within...it sounds like a whisper and it looks like white snow. Beauty understands its value, and she leaves it to be protected by the King until He gives her the nod that this young man understands. I want the very same things for your teens.

Treading Tips

Know the struggles common among teens and don't put off having the hard conversations with your own teen. You'll never regret the conversations, but you will regret those never had.

Set boundaries for your teens and communicate why they are important. Example: *You can't be at our house or your girlfriend or boyfriend's home when parents are not there. It creates too much temptation.*

Prepare your teens for the ridicule they will likely face from their peers if they choose to remain sexually pure. Help them develop ways to deal with it.

Be confident in your calling as a parent. You are the gatekeeper of your home. Your teen needs you to take your position seriously.

Be aware of what devices your child is using and sexting trends. (See Technology Chapter.)

Know your child's friends, friends of friends, and parents of friends. You want to be aware of what other friends are allowed to do in their homes. Their rules may vary greatly from your own.

Explain to your teen that Satan desires to steal the blessing and beauty of sex from them and their spouse. But the Lord has written for them a beautiful love story.

Read their text messages. Have your teen turn in all of their electronics to you at night.

Use filters and search to see if your teen is struggling with pornography—deal with it quickly.

We should know our children's friends and their parents. We should consider it a warning sign when you have a child who constantly wants to go to a particular friend's home. When I was growing up, especially when I was a teenager, if we went to someone else's house it was because we could get away with more at that friend's home than we could at ours. When at my friends' homes, I could stay out later, have boys over, drink without getting caught, or watch inappropriate movies and television channels. Let's face it, as a teenage girl the hair products alone make staying the night away a chore...there must be some kind of a "payoff" to make it worth all the effort. If your child *always* wants to go to Johnny's house, that should raise a red flag and should make you question what goes on at Johnny's. Have an understanding with your children that if you go to Susie's house today, next time Susie needs to come to your house. You need to know their friends and their friends need to know you.

Remember that sex is progressive. If we allow the progression to begin too young, we are simply fighting a losing battle. Consider the activities you are allowing.

Be open an honest about pornography. Give your teen tools to deal with that temptation in a way that honors God.
Teach your young men how to pursue young women with honor and your daughter how to maintain dignity and modesty in the pursuit.

Life Preservers

Let the king be enthralled by your beauty; honor him, for he is your lord..

Psalm 45:11

Do not conform to the pattern of this world, but be transformed by the renewing of your mind. Then you will be able to test and approve what God's will is—his good, pleasing and perfect will.

Romans 12:2

But you are a chosen people, a royal priesthood, a holy nation, God's special possession, that you may declare the praises of him who called you out of darkness into his wonderful light.

1 Peter 2:9

But in your hearts revere Christ as Lord. Always be prepared to give an answer to everyone who asks you to give the reason for the hope that you have. But do this with gentleness and respect, keeping a clear conscience, so that those who speak maliciously against your good behavior in Christ may be ashamed of their slander. For it is better, if it is God's will, to suffer for doing good than for doing evil.

1 Peter 3:15-17

Flee from sexual immorality. All other sins a person commits are outside the body, but whoever sins sexually, sins against their own body.

1 Corinthians 6:18

No temptation has overtaken you except what is common to mankind. And God is faithful; he will not let you be tempted beyond what you can bear. But when you are tempted, he will also provide a way out so that you can endure it.

1 Corinthians 10:13

It is God's will that you should be sanctified: that you should avoid sexual immorality; that each of you should learn to control your own body in a way that is holy and honorable, not in passionate lust like the pagans, who do not know God;

1 Thessalonians 4:3-5

Technology

"According to the latest Kaiser Family Foundation data, 8-to-18 year olds are spending more than 50 hours a week with digital media. That's more than a full workweek. Are e-mail, mp3s and the web affecting your child's brain?"[5]

*"Today, **8-18 year-olds devote an average of 7 hours and 38 minutes*** (7:38) to using entertainment media across a typical day (more than 53 *hours a week). And because they spend so much of that time 'media multitasking' (using more than one medium at a time), they actually manage to pack a total of 10 hours and 45 minutes (10:45) worth of media content into those 7½ hours."*[6]

Wow. Can you image that our kids are spending that much time with digital devices? I know as a mom it can seem so overwhelming to keep up with not only our children's activities and events, but also their friends, lingo, and now all that they are faced with online and via social networking. But seeing these statistics, how can we not educate ourselves and communicate with our kids about the dangers and situations that can arise?

I want to begin by saying that having a close relationship with your children from the beginning is critical; you need this in order to talk about any subject. Your children are tuning in to something. They are wired up, synced up, connected to, and interacting with a very large community. Shouldn't they be tuned in to the Father? Synced up with your family and your values?

If the norm in your home is to make small talk until everyone once again finds themselves submerged in work, technology, or friends, then it will be difficult for you to try and have open communication about any isolated topic. It is all about relationships.

In my opinion, the biggest obstacle in our families today is isolation. Somehow our culture has convinced us that it is okay for us to all live separate lives, that teens need to have constant contact with their peer group and could care less what you have to say. That is simply not the case. Your children are a part of your family and you need to function as such.

There needs to be limits set on the amount of time spent on game systems, phones, iPads, and computers, or simply just alone in their rooms. Interact with each other, spend time together doing things like the dishes, working in the yard, or going on a hike. The only way to have a relationship with our kids is *to have a relationship with our kids.*

Social media

We asked our Lifeguards, "What do you consider to be the biggest struggle for teens in the thirteen to nineteen-year age group?" There responses included identity, comparison, sexual temptation, self-image, and fitting in.

Do you see the train wreck waiting to happen? We have 80% of teens highly engaged on social media sites like Facebook, Twitter, Vine, Pinterest, and Instagram who are also dealing with issues like identity, comparison, sexual temptation, self-image, and peer pressure. What a dangerous situation.

I am not saying that all teens should be forbidden to engage in social media, because attempting this is simply unrealistic. However, balance and boundaries are imperative. How and when did we as a culture decide this kind of fixation or addiction should be considered permissible or normal? We have young people struggling with their own self-image because they are reading the high points of their peers' lives in a Facebook stream. We have all heard stories of young people devastated to see pictures of a party they were not invited to on Instagram or Facebook and Twitter posts of a girl who has made out with the boy her friend is dating. Young people compare themselves to the class president, class favorite, valedictorian, and blue-chip athlete. Everyone's lives look more perfect and glamorous on their Twitter feed than it does in real life.

Young men are posting videos and comments about their sexual encounters with young women, and photos and videos of teens drinking and partying are commonplace. Social media has taken the regrettable, embarrassing moments experienced by teens of fifteen years ago in the presence of twenty people at a party and magnified it into a humiliating display for literally millions. These images can and will come back to haunt them. Universities and employers often research a person's social media accounts before granting admittance or offering a position. Can you fathom the implications of that on your child's future?

As parents, we need to set the example. We, too, are consumed with social media. Eighty-two percent of parents under age of forty say they use social networking sites and 61% of parents over age forty say they do too.[7] Our lives are being broadcast over the Internet as well. We are the ones more concerned about posting a picture of our cute son in his football jersey than actually watching the game. Be aware of what *you* share online. Put down your phone, step away from the computer, and spend quality time with your family. There is absolutely no substitute for spending time together as a family. Make memories together. Time goes so quickly.

I want to savor every moment I have with my family. I remember sitting on the couch last Christmas with Jake and Madi and realizing I only have six more Christmases with Madi living our home and only four left with Jake. As a mom, I am simply not willing to give over all the priceless time I have with my children to be consumed by Facebook and a cell phone. What ever happened to enjoying the great outdoors or family dinners at the table? I am not sure where our appreciation for sacred family times have gone, but I am quite sure that we as a society would do well to find it.

Cell phones

In my humble opinion, parents should be more thoughtful about the appropriate age for their teen to begin using a cell phone. Without exception, when I make that statement someone in the crowd will say, "How will I know when to pick them up from events?" It almost makes me chuckle because I didn't have a cell phone until Brian and I were married. Funny thing is, my parents always picked me up from practice or games with no problem at all.

In the world we live, you can rest assured that there will be at least fifteen cell phones within arm's reach in case of emergency. A solution that has worked well in our home, even when my guys were thirteen and fourteen years old, is to have an extra phone that belongs to no one in particular. For example, if my son has an away game and will be late getting home, he would take the extra phone. If my daughter is riding bikes with her friends, she would take the extra phone. But the majority of the time, it is plugged in to charge in our room. Since the phone doesn't belong to them, they aren't able to give the number out to friends or get into any trouble on it, by the way, it isn't a smart phone.

Another problem with younger teens having cell phones is that friends and peers have complete and constant access to them. It was once the norm for boys to call girls and not vice versa. Wow, doesn't that seem like a lifetime ago? The Father fashioned men to pursue women. Young men don't have to worry with that today. They have ten girls blowing up their cell phones before they finish a snack after school.

Girls remain the most enthusiastic texters, with a median of 100 texts a day in 2011, compared with fifty for boys the same age.[8] Many young women are pursuing young men in today's culture, but we simply were not designed that way. The truth is that the girls who have their own life and interests are the ones young men find interesting. Sure, he will take what he can from the girl offering it, but in the end, it will be the young lady with a head on her shoulders and something going for herself that he will pursue.

Recently I was visiting with a mom about her daughter. She said that after sending her children to bed around 10:00 p.m. and then heading there herself, she woke up around 1:00 a.m., headed down the hall to the rest room, and discovered her daughter's bedroom light on. The mom went into the girl's room to discover that she was on her cell phone with a boy. The mother told her in no uncertain terms to get off the phone and stay off. The mother went back to bed. Waking up again at 3:00 a.m., she found her daughter on the phone again! The mother could not believe the daughter would be so defiant. (I know that all of you are thinking the same thing I was thinking: why was the daughter allowed to go to bed with her phone?) If we are honest, we will all admit that if you get a text at 1:00 a.m. and your phone is near your bed, as a forty-something adult, you will check your phone. What on earth would make us think that our teens could resist? We have to wise up and tune in ourselves.

Teens will text things they would never say verbally. It removes inhibition, and that can lead to all kinds of trouble. Teens are more likely to bully, send sexual text messages, disrespect authority, or gossip about their friends via a text message than they would be in face-to-face or verbal conversations. It lends itself to too much anonymity.

Whatever the benefits of giving younger teens a cell phone are, they are far outweighed by the possible violations of their innocence and trouble they may find themselves in. Be very sure you are ready to begin the process of a cell phone before you buy the phone. Consider the pros and cons.

Let's Ask the Lifeguards

If parents set unpopular guidelines for technology with our teens, what should we remember?

It does depend on the relationship, but as humans we do

want the rules. We need you to keep your word. We may not like it, but it is predictable. (Christian)

You do need to give them responsibility when possible and safe. It will allow your teen to gain more of your respect and help them to earn more freedoms. (Christian)

You want to raise young adults, so you have to give them some responsibility so that they grow and learn responsibility. The goal is to raise adults. (Andrew)

You have set such a high goal for your kids, it is important to help them with a road map. This is how you get to your goal. Your kids trust you and then they see that if they obey they can achieve their goals. They see the purpose and the payoff. (Jace)

If you are moving in the right direction, we are all about it. We are your biggest fans, but we will be your biggest nightmare if you get off track. Relationship is a big deal. (Candy)

Scary Technology Trends

Ask.fm – A social networking website where users can create an account under total anonymity and ask anyone any question they can dream up. As you can imagine, these questions can quickly become sexual. Because teens believe there is true anonymity, they feel free to ask or say anything. Ask.fm has apps for most devices with many features, including the video answer program, in which users can tag each other. With over 70 million users and 30 million questions daily, Ask.fm has been linked to many cyber-bullying cases, even terrorism.[9]

Snapchat – This iPhone app allows users to send photos that will "self-destruct" within ten seconds, encouraging kids to feel more comfortable "sexting" with peers. Once the recipient opens the pic, the timer starts, and the image self-destructs once the time has expired. This app gives kids a false sense of security in sending inappropriate pictures or texts; however, damage can still be done within a specified time frame. The recipient is able to take a photo of their screen with the text is showing. This creates a problem when that recipient forwards or shows others. Talk to your child about the dangers of sending risky photos.

Snapchat Stories is a newer feature of Snapchat where the user can add "snaps" together to create a story. The stories stay live for twenty-four hours and then self-destruct like Snapchat.

Chatroulette – Log into the site and people are randomly connected—over video, audio, and text—with another person logged into the site. Texas Attorney General Greg Abbott has issued a consumer alert warning parents to keep their children away from video chat web site Chatroulette. One estimate from the Texas Attorney General's investigation is that nearly half of the people found on the site were behaving in inappropriate ways. (Just what you would want your middle schooler to be party to, I'm sure.) An analysis of Chatroulette traffic earlier this year by RJMetrics provided the following results: 89% of single people were male, 11% female.[10] In fact, you are more likely to encounter nobody at all than a single female, and twice as likely to encounter a sign requesting female nudity than you are to encounter actual female nudity. One in eight sessions result in something R-rated or worse, including explicit nudity, and lewd acts.[11]

Puff or Blow Skirt – Beware Peeping Toms! Although these apps are not full nudity, your children can blow a lady's dress up, literally. Once downloaded, the user can blow into the microphone or use a swiping motion to lift the skirts of girls in pictures. While *most* are wearing underwear, it still sends the wrong message. Do we really want our children participating in something like this as a joke or to pass the time?

Poof by Cydia – With one touch, *Poof* makes apps disappear before parents' prying eyes, allowing young users of "jailbroken" iPhones to virtually hide apps they don't want you to see. All your little tech genius needs to do is open Poof and select which app he or she wants hidden, and you'll never know it's there.

KiK Messenger – This kicky app for all types of smartphones is a mini social network. Similar to iChat or Google Chat, users can talk to multiple people, upload pictures, files, and even send built-in greeting cards or sketched pictures. The reviews read like dating ads, with users looking to get to know more people. This app has become a way for teenagers to sext with strangers.[12]

Make sure you talk with your kids about the dangers of "meeting" people online!

There certainly is a lot to consider, and we have only scratched the surface. It is our job as parents to be informed. The sad truth is that much of the material you as an adult would view on some of these sites or apps could cause a problem for you. Yet, we are allowing our children to access them even if unbeknownst to us.

I know that we cannot shelter our kids from technology. They are going to use technology, and technology is not intrinsically "bad." However, we allow our children to have cell phones, iPads, and social media accounts far too early. We allow our children to be put into adult situations before they are equipped to handle them. Filters do help. Parents having an understanding about the devices, apps, and programs their children use is crucial. But using filters and gaining knowledge simply will not protect them completely.

I want to encourage you. You are the parent of your child or teen. Don't fall to pressure from our culture. You decide what is okay in your home. You set the boundaries. Remember, parenting is about your relationship with the Father. If you are obedient to Him when it comes to setting boundaries with your kids, you can't go wrong!

Treading Tips

GET ACCESS: If you allow your teen to use social media or the Internet, you need to have access to all of their passwords and logins. Over half of all 8-18 year olds (52%) say they have rules about what they can do on the computer.[13] We must set our children up for success; this means giving them the appropriate boundaries. Christian said during our discussion, "A teenager doesn't have enough discernment (to be free to use social media). They don't understand how random thoughts and images can affect their mind." Ask yourself if you are confident that your boundaries and systems would allow you to catch your teen's questionable behavior early on.

Check your child's Facebook, Twitter, Instagram, Vine, Snapchat, etc. You would be wise to look at the pages of their friends as well. You won't have to look far to see what takes place in their world. Fifty-nine percent of parents with teens who use social networking sites have talked with their children due to concern about something posted to their profiles or accounts. (That translates to 46% of parents of all online teens.)[14] Having these conversations early prevent worse situations from happening. Be brave, be aware, know what is going on and don't be afraid to address it.

Use Resources. I have provided a list of programs below that track social media. You link your children's accounts, and the programs will send you reports on risky behavior and flag inappropriate language. Obviously, having access to your child's account would eliminate the need for this, but you may still find these helpful:

www.theiphonemom.com
www.theonlinemom.com
www.connectsafely.org
www.socialsheild.com

Ask the Lord to give you directions with boundaries and commit to abide by the set boundaries.

Both the iPod Touch and iPhone require an iTunes account for set up and to allow the user to download music, movies, apps, or other content from the iTunes Store. I recommend setting this up immediately with a password that is private to you and not shared with your child. This way, in order to download anything, whether it be a song or an app, your child will have to approach you to plug in the password, allowing you to have full knowledge of what they are adding.

A passcode is a great way to protect an iPod Touch, iPhone, or iPad. It's a security code that you or your child will have to enter every time you want to use the device. This is helpful in case your child loses the device—you wouldn't want a stranger to get access to any family information, pictures, or phone numbers. Make sure to use a passcode both you and your child can remember.

Install age appropriate apps. The app store has lots of fun programs that are so helpful for entertaining kiddos when you're traveling, need some distraction, or are looking to interact with them.

Uninstall apps that come with the iPhone that may be inappropriate. I would disable Safari. There is no built-in content filter on the devices and none on this web browser.

Use the extra family phone.

Life Preservers

Finally, brothers and sisters, whatever is true, whatever is noble, whatever is right, whatever is pure, whatever is lovely, whatever is admirable—if anything is excellent or praiseworthy—think about such things.

Philippians 4:8

But I tell you that anyone who looks at a woman lustfully has already committed adultery with her in his heart.

Matthew 5:28

Do not conform to the pattern of this world, but be transformed by the renewing of your mind. All who sin apart from the law will also perish apart from the law, and all who sin under the law will be judged by the law.

Romans 2:12

My Teen is Struggling with Homosexuality

Our culture has accepted two huge lies. The first is that if you disagree with someone's lifestyle, you must fear or hate them. The second is that to love someone means you agree with everything they believe or do. Both are nonsense. You don't have to compromise convictions to be compassionate.
Rick Warren

Likely the most emotional issue we discussed with the Lifeguards was homosexuality. There wasn't a dry eye in the house. Several topics really struck a chord with the kids and with me over the course of our time together and this was certainly one of them. It was very apparent to all of us that these difficult topics are the point of pain for people, often for people we love—they are not simply "issues" or bullet points on a page. They're not just debates or trending controversies; they are heartbreak and victory. And homosexuality tops the list.

Each of the Lifeguards knew someone personally who struggled or currently struggles with homosexuality. Does the local church offer help to parents dealing with a teen facing this temptation? The consensus of the group seemed to be that the church appears unprepared and is often silent on the topic. It can seem as though many in the body of believers are afraid of discussing sexuality, let alone homosexuality. Though some churches, mine being one, will still contend that homosexuality is a sin and that it is not a behavior honoring of God, are we as believers prepared to offer help to people struggling with it? There seems to be support groups for almost every sinful issue under the sun, but you will be hard pressed to find one for homosexuality.

Another point of contention is that taking a stand against homosexuality often gets you pegged as a bigot. Our Lifeguards have found that there really is no way to make an argument against homosexuality, certainly on college campuses, without being looked at as a judgmental Bible-thumper. There must be an approach Christians can take in discussions about the spiritual consequences of sin without appearing harsh, judgmental, or self-righteous. How can we practically love the person yet stand against the sin?

The Bible describes sexual sin as a sin against your own body (1 Corinthians 6:18). Homosexuality certainly falls in to this category. It is a sin against God and a sin against the person engaging in the act.

Is homosexuality genetic? Are people born that way? There were definite, strong feelings on both sides of that argument. Personally I would like to believe people are not *born* gay. I do believe that we all may have a higher propensity for weakness or struggle in the area of one particular sin over another. In the same sense, some people are more prone to become alcoholics, others to be sexually promiscuous. Some people may be more prone towards homosexuality and some toward lying, yet that doesn't mean we were *born* that way.

We are born into a fallen world. We are born with a propensity to sin. We are descendants of Adam. We have a sin nature. However, our purpose is not to determine the cause of homosexuality or debate same sex marriage. Our purpose is to throw a life preserver to the parent of a teenager dealing with homosexuality.

Let's Ask the Lifeguards

In your opinion, how are Christians and our culture addressing the issue of homosexuality?

✎ On the college campus, unlike abortion, if you don't support gay marriage you are looked at like, *Oh, you intolerant, bigot Chris-*

tian. How can you not love and accept people? You get portrayed as the bad person if you don't agree with it. I can give a list of things and say you aren't born gay. If you give a Biblical response, they just say, "I am not a Christian and I don't believe in that." What I have learned is that your argument cannot be Biblical. (Jace)

We want alcoholics to take responsibility and admit they have a problem and when they do we have support and resources to help them. But when someone struggling with homosexual feelings needs help, often the church is terrified, and we don't know what to do. Dealing with homosexuality should be likened to dealing with other struggles. Acknowledge without minimizing that the person has the struggle and show them what the Bible says and how to fight that with scripture. Their feelings are legitimate. They aren't making it up. (Christian)

Everybody in here would say that we struggle being tempted sexually. Something that gives us hope is knowing that, if we are pure and if we wait, one day God will have a special person for us. If we can stay pure we will have that. We can hope for that. What if homosexuals don't have that to hope for unless God takes that desire away? And yes, we know He can but sometimes He doesn't. I have someone very close to me who has dealt with this, and it has almost destroyed his family. This young man knew there was something different about him when he was ten. He wasn't sexually abused or unloved but his whole life he felt different. He grew up in a Christian home, and because of this struggle he felt hated. Until I knew about this issue, I was the worst. I would say fag, gay, and queer and joke about that. But you never know the damage that does to someone. Every time we say those things, we rip them apart. I believe that homosexuality is wrong, and I am not sure why it is here. I know we live in a fallen world. I am not saying homosexuality is a disease, but there are a lot of people who don't want to be the way they are. They know this is wrong, but if all we do as Christians is say this is wrong...they know that. All we are doing is separating ourselves and pushing them away. A gay person knows that *If I choose to follow Christ and He doesn't take this desire away*...they know they will never have a romantic love relationship. It is easy for us to say this is what you should do, but you have to have a heart and understanding of what that means practically. We are called to be bold, and we have to address the issue, but we have to be better. Don't let your opinion negate your ability to love the person. (Andrew)

I don't think this issue is at the top of the list of issues facing our country. I think that there is enough evidence that this isn't just a choice; there is research showing it is genetic or their home life. They don't make this choice just for attention that leads to being persecuted and ripped apart. (Luke)

I have a big heart for this issue. When I was fourteen, I had a friend, and I was the first person she told about this struggle. I didn't know how to handle it; I think I was in denial. I pushed her away and it is hard because I wish I could go back and show her love. I think she felt judged by me and by the church, and it pushed her away from God. So, I would like the church to be able to help people with this. I don't believe it is right, but it is a struggle. You *will* struggle—the temptation isn't the sin; it's acting on it. As Christians, we need to show love to them, and I wish I had been able to do that with my friend. It is not going to be easy because they will feel different. If we can learn to see the people, maybe we can impact their lives. God does love them. (Kaylee)

I have to make a comment. This issue is destroying our families. We don't know why, but it makes us have horrible doubts in our faith. Why would God create someone with a broken leg and send him to hell for limping? He wouldn't. That doesn't make sense. That's not the God I know. If I know the God up there, I know they can't be made that way. Otherwise, God isn't who He says He is. There can't be a gay gene. You can't pass on a gene that can't be passed on. I do agree that we can have a predisposition for certain sin and we are all tempted in different ways. Just look at the different ways guys and girls are tempted. Girls are more tempted to gossip and guys to look at girls in the wrong way. They are both sins. There has to be an answer. God can change you, but you have to fight it every day. I am not saying it is easy. If they come out of that, they would have a huge platform. (Jace)

To say that people are born this way or that if they have enough faith, they will get through this...both steal hope. God didn't take Paul's thorn away. He struggled. I completely agree the temptation isn't the sin, the action is. (Andrew)

If Christians only say "it is wrong," we aren't telling homosexuals something they don't already know. Have a heart for people and love them. We are called not to judge, but to love, regardless of someone's choices or actions. As Christians, we are called to love them and legitimately reveal Jesus to them by our actions and words. (Andrew)

How does a Christian family deal with having a child who struggles with homosexuality?

For the Lifeguards, the most heart-wrenching part of our discussion on homosexuality came when I asked, "How does a Christian family deal with having a child who struggles with homosexuality?" How do we continue to be loving and inclusive of that family member without condoning their behavior? What a very difficult, lonely road to walk. As a parent, I can only imagine the heartbreak involved. Having a sibling facing homosexuality would be difficult as well. Sin hurts families. It hurts the people who are caught in that trap. There are no easy answers.

Speaking as a mother who, like most moms I know, wants so many things for my children, I can say that I desire for my children to live life to the fullest. I want them to experience adventure and excitement. I pray often that they will laugh until they cry and that they cry from deep within for hurting people. I want them to find a spouse who will love them, journey with them, laugh with them, and support them. I want them to be happy and fulfilled. I want them to live out the calling the Lord has on their life with passion. Truly, my deepest desire is that they love the Lord with all of their heart, soul, and might.

Brian and I have experienced many rough sea moments in this long swim of raising teenagers. Nothing could have prepared us mentally, physically, emotionally, or spiritually. It has truly been a sink-or-swim kind of experience much of the time, and we certainly do not have a perfect family. But I have never been the momma of a teen struggling with homosexuality and to say that I "feel their pain" would be insincere and ridiculous. However, I have a precious friend who has strapped her life vest tight and paddled out into the deep to lock arms with her son and swim for shore in the high seas of homosexuality.

I decided to see if she would throw us a life preserver, and she did. Here are some questions that I posed along with her answers. (I have left her answers untouched. I want to be sure that she is allowed her voice, and I don't want to make it mine.)

- How did you discover that your son struggled with homosexuality?

  Our son was just over sixteen when he admitted he was gay. He had been "unsettled" for a long time, but we didn't know why. We thought he would feel better when he had some increased freedom associated with being able to drive. That was not the case and keeping curfew became a problem. He flopped on my bed one day while I was doing something as if he wanted to talk. I asked why he was so unhappy. I gave him a list of options, trying to get him to open up. For some reason, I listed "are you gay?" as one of the options. I still have little idea why I asked that question. His answer was "that's it." I wasn't even sure what was "it," as I asked many things in quick succession.

Needless to say, that changed my life forever. Looking back, we did have one warning of this prior to his admission. My husband had found a shredded story with a homosexual theme several years earlier. We did ask him about the paper at the time. He denied being homosexual. I was relieved and said something stupid like I was so glad because I would kill myself if I thought he was gay. I know many gay people and would not wish that lifestyle for my precious son. Still.... it is obvious why he didn't tell me for a few years. He didn't want to be the death of his mom! He begged me to keep this a secret, as he didn't want anyone to find out. I don't keep secrets from my spouse, so this was a terrible time of sadness and loneliness. Finally, I had to tell my husband or lose my sanity. We both had to wrestle with the news then, but I was no longer alone to cope.

- Were there any resources available to you as Christian parents to help you in dealing with the situation? If so, what was most helpful?

We found very few books that we thought were helpful. This was several years ago, so maybe there is better information out there now. The only book I could relate to is very old from Barbara Johnson called, "Where Does a Mother Go to Resign?" Doesn't the title summarize it all? Mothering is tough! It was written in the eighties, so much of the language is outdated. It still helped me because it was an honest mother hurting after discovering her son was gay. She chose to love her son no matter what. We found much of the Christian literature trite and hurtful. I don't believe this is a simple problem, so simple solutions are more irritating than helpful.

- How did your friends and family support you?

  Our family has been great. My son is loved just as much now, if not more than before. One family member has a hard time accepting my son's partner into his home. My friends who know my son haven't changed their opinion of him, as they know what a great person he is. Many people choose not to ask about him when I see them, however, which is because they are busy or trying not to embarrass me or are just uncomfortable.

- Have you found a way to stay close to your son in adulthood?

  We still see our son a lot. He needs our love more than ever. We have at least one meal a week together. He makes the effort to connect and so do we.

- How did this struggle affect your nuclear family?

  We all struggled a lot at first. It's still not easy. My husband had a harder time than I did. He had more guilt that he should have done something differently. Our son has become an atheist, which has frightened us much more than his being gay.

  I do think we are better people for having a gay son and brother. We are much more humble. 1+1 does not always equal 2. We are less likely to throw stones at someone who is hurting. We are much more compassionate. We listen more and give answers less.

- Did this struggle have an effect on your relationship with Christ? How so?

  I had to decide if Christ was trustworthy. I had sown "good seed" but was getting something I hadn't asked for. Somehow I saw Christianity as a guarantee of good outcome: I do my part and God is supposed to do His. Training my child did not get him to go the way I thought he ought. I felt betrayed. I suspect people who get lung cancer without smoking feel the same way.

  God was sweet to gently wait while I questioned His goodness. "Is God Really in Control" by Jerry Bridges helped immensely to settle the legs underneath me. I chose to believe several precepts of the book. 1) God is always in control, even when it doesn't seem like it. Nothing takes him by surprise. 2) He works all things out for all people at the same time for everyone's best. I chose to believe that God was going to make my son and my husband and my other children better because He is loving and able to bring good out of this situation. I no longer have a cookie cutter relationship with God. I have wrestled with Him and decided that He still has the "words of life" even when things don't turn out like I thought they were supposed to.

Pretty powerful from one mom's heart, hopefully to yours. In addition to asking my friend to answer these questions, I also requested that she write a letter to a parent who may be facing this same situation. She generously obliged, and I invite you to read the following:

Dear mom or dad who has a gay son or lesbian daughter,

I am sure you are hoping that I will have some clear answers on why people are gay. The truth is that I don't believe a perfectly satisfying answer is out there. It seems to me that we are a long way from the Gar-

den of Eden. Many things happen on earth now that were not meant to happen in a perfect world where we walked in the cool of the afternoon with God. People get cancer and suffer from oppressive governments and many other things that are God-allowed. I am not saying God causes them to be gay, but He has filtered this through His hands and allowed this into our lives.

What does all this mean to you?

I would suggest that you first be careful with the words you use when talking to your child. It is quite likely that they are hurting, and you need to be their safety net, even if you feel very unsteady yourself. Gay teenagers have a high rate of suicide, and we don't want to push them over the edge of hopelessness. Your unconditional love is needed more than ever. You will have to deal with the chaos in your mind, but you cannot and should not do it without filters in front of your child.

As parents, we need to do the best we can to raise our children, and we need to take responsibility for our shortcomings. I do not believe, however, that it is our fault that our children are gay. Stop beating yourself up over this. Self-blame does not allow you to move forward in loving your child.

Surround yourself with supportive people. It is likely that no one will really understand, as this is a difficult area. We Christians tend to have reasons that make sense to us why people are gay. I haven't found most of these reasons very helpful.

It is likely that people will be trying to help "fix" the situation with your child as they did with my husband and me, but it made us feel more frustrated and added to our shame and confusion. I would recommend that you take what is helpful and reject what is not. I believe that people genuinely loved our family and were trying to help.

Of course, there are some who leave the homosexual lifestyle. You need to love your child whether they remain gay or not. The real issue is that we want our children to love the Lord. It is very hard for gay people to find a way to stay near the God of the Bible. I do not believe that the Bible allows for an active homosexual life. This makes it difficult for these men and women when they did not want to be gay in the first place. I do not believe that we should go against the Bible, but we ought to offer compassion to the fact that our children find themselves in a difficult situation. We have to remind them that, despite all else, Jesus is crazy in love with them. Only Jesus' love can make a difference.

If a mom or dad is reading this note and doesn't have a gay or lesbian child, I would ask that you react to your friends who do with compassion. They will covet your prayers for themselves and their children, but be careful about the advice you will give. They will appreciate you not running away from the family and your continued love for their child just as before you found out they were homosexual. The Christian community is known for being haters of the homosexual community. Of course that is not correct, but it is still the perception. I believe we will have to work harder to reach these young men and women by being even more patient and Christ-like. We need to do the best we can to show them Christ's love in whatever way we can. For the readers of this, it may just be one-on-one with your child or the child of your friend. The Holy Spirit can give you some creative ways to reach out.

My son is married now. He and his spouse know we wish they were not gay. They also know that we are much more concerned that they choose not to love God than that they are homosexual. Nothing is easy in this situation. We try to live our lives as transparently as possible in a way that makes Jesus desirable. Salvation is His business.

Blessings to you. Keep loving your kid. They are still great kids. Keep loving God.

One day we will meet in the cool of the garden....

I am tearful reading her heart penned for you. It was difficult for her to find words and to open some of those wounds in her own family to serve you. However, for those of you grasping for a life preserver, this is hope in the form of a life vest.

I have a family member who lives a homosexual lifestyle. I was very close to this person as a child, and she was one of my closest friends as a teenager and young adult. I don't see her often now because our paths just don't cross much. Life becomes so busy. As I have asked the Lord about her and her circumstances, a few of her life situations come to mind. She spent her childhood years with a chronically ill parent and then had a tragic loss in her late teens. She is very successful in a certain activity, and in this particular pastime there is an acceptance for homosexually. The situation became common in her life and it became easier for the lifestyle to be something she was comfortable with. I have had direct conversations with her about it, and she knows my thoughts on the lifestyle. What is important is that she knows what the Word claims regarding homosexuality and that I love her deeply. I cherish my years with her.

As a group, the Lifeguards and I finally came to the place of saying that healing is where we should put our focus. Everyone in our group agreed that no sin is any worse than another. However, one cannot debate the fact that the Bible is clear about homosexuality being a sin. We all struggle with a sin nature. We *all* struggle.

So, at this point we are exactly where we claimed many churches are at the beginning of our chapter—acknowledging that homosexuality is a sin, realizing that our heart is to love people first and well, but not really offering any practical help or advice. If we would agree that sin is sin and that homosexuality is a sexual sin in the same way that sex outside of marriage is a sexual sin, then we have common ground.

Sexual Purity in Homosexuality

As the parent of a teenager, how do we address sexual sin? "That is why a man leaves his father and mother and is united to his wife, and they become one flesh." (Genesis 2:24) Sex is a beautiful gift from the Father for married couples. Marriage is a religious institution and is between one man and one woman. Sex is reserved for marriage. That means that if our teenagers are attracted to another person, be that heterosexually or homosexually, they do not have license to be sexually involved until they are married, in the Biblical sense of the word.

Many heterosexual people never marry and are thus called to a life of sexual abstinence. I believe the same is true for people who have a propensity toward homosexuality. One cannot be married by the Biblical definition to someone of the same sex and, in this case, sex outside of marriage is still the sin—the requirement being sexual abstinence.

I recently heard Beth Moore say, "I can't make people behave." We simply do not have control of our children and their choices. They make choices we would rather they not make about many different issues and often. However, we have control over what *we* choose and where we set the boundaries for our families and ourselves. Sexual purity is an expectation for our teens. Is it difficult? Yes. (Ok, that is the understatement of the decade!) But does the fact that it is difficult negate the truth? Sadly, no. This is a battlefield we all fight on regardless of whether our teen is attracted to people of the same or opposite sex.

We must have open conversation with our teenagers about purity and why the Lord has called us to self-control. We have to help our teens set healthy boundaries. We need to teach them to think ahead and set clear expectations in all of their relationships, where are the lines that they will not cross?

When two people engage in sexual intercourse, a soul-tie is formed. Once that line has been crossed in any relationship outside of marriage the battle intensifies because we have given the enemy a foothold. Equipping our teenagers to battle for their sexuality is one of our most important callings in this day and age. Talking, praying, searching the scriptures, and setting healthy boundaries and guidelines for them are all critical steps to sexual purity. Our families must base our lives on His Word. It is the only unchanging, immovable, constant anchor that we have in the chaos of life. It holds. The question is, will we?

These waters are the scariest we've seen, but from this momma to you, we will not turn back and we will not give in and drown here. There are simply struggles and difficulties we cannot save our children from and miles of these oceans that we cannot swim for them. We have to keep the life preserver of His Word strapped tight around us so that we can be a hand for our teens to reach for as they struggle to keep their head above these waves.

How does one bridge the gap between accepting that homosexuality is a sin and loving our child with the same self-sacrificing, unconditional, and really indescribable love of a parent? The fact remains that homosexuality is a sin no worse than other sin. All sin causes us to be separated from God. It breaks my heart, but it broke His too, so He didn't just create a bridge; He became the very bridge that can make the difference. Jesus chose to set His perfect divine feet on our dusty shore so that He could literally stretch out His arms to save us. We don't have to figure out how we can maneuver this water to make it to shore; we simply reach for the Lifeguard. He takes care of the rescuing.

Struggle well. Work out your faith with fear and trembling. Whether or not He delivers us from whatever thorn is in our own flesh, we must chase Him. Our focus must be on serving Him. Homosexuality is difficult. It's difficult for everyone involved. As believers, we are to love people and come alongside them in their attempt to struggle well.

And what does the Lord require of you?
To act justly and to love mercy and to walk humbly
with your God.

Micah 6:8

Treading Tips

Love well. It is truly the compassion and goodness of Christ that draws our children to Him. Loving your child *and* maintaining your commitment to the Lord is possible.

Scripture memory is so important. The Word of God is our sword. We must hide God's Word in our heart. Scripture helps us all in difficult times. Focusing on God's Word reminds us of the benefits of purity and of His promises.

Set boundaries for your family. Explain the Biblical lines you will not cross. Your teen ultimately will make their own choices about how they will live their life, but you have the authority to decide how you will live yours. You decide what will or will not be allowed in your home if your teen decides to live a homosexual lifestyle.

Stop trying to figure out what you did "wrong" as a parent that may have caused or influenced your child toward homosexuality. Looking forward and focusing on how you might help your teen in their struggle is far more beneficial.

Listen to your teen who struggles with homosexuality. It is ok to bawl your eyes out. Don't minimize their struggle, but realize you can't fix it for them. Just lock arms and spend some time resting on the waves...just being together.

If you have a teen who struggles with homosexuality, find a Christian support group in your area who can come alongside you and your family.

Life Preservers

Do not have sexual relations with a man as one does with a woman; that is detestable.

Leviticus 18:22

That is why a man leaves his father and mother and is united to his wife, and they become one flesh.

Genesis 2:24

Therefore God gave them over in the sinful desires of their hearts to sexual impurity for the degrading of their bodies with one another. They exchanged the truth about God for a lie, and worshiped and served created things rather than the Creator—who is forever praised. Amen.

Romans 1:24-25

Finally, all of you, be like-minded, be sympathetic, love one another, be compassionate and humble.

1 Peter 3:8

And the Lord said, "I will cause all my goodness to pass in front of you, and I will proclaim my name, the Lord, in your presence. I will have mercy on whom I will have mercy, and I will have compassion on whom I will have compassion.

Exodus 33:19

The Lord is gracious and righteous; our God is full of compassion.

Psalm 116:5

Pro-Life & Pro-Choice

Let us say "Yes" to life and not death. Let us say "Yes" to freedom and not enslavement to the many idols of our time. In a word, let us say "Yes" to the God who is love, life and freedom, and who never disappoints.
Pope Francis

Being pro-life or pro-choice is an interesting discussion when I think about it. I've seen it from just about every seat in the house. I am a pro-life speaker and am committed to the pro-life side of this argument, but I have listened to people from a political standpoint, from a religious standpoint, from a liberal standpoint, and from a conservative standpoint all debate their sides of the issue. I have had the privilege to join young ladies standing literally on holy ground as they make a decision about an unplanned pregnancy. Often times, their decision really has little to do with whether they consider themselves to be "pro-life" or "pro-choice." For them, in a moment, it simply becomes *my choice*.

In 2013 our centers saw more than eighty pregnant women considering abortion, and seventy-three of them chose to carry their babies. There is hope.

I have been the young woman facing the dilemma of being pregnant, unwed, and in high school. I have been the mother of an unmarried son determining with his girlfriend whether or not they would carry their baby (I might add that my precious grandson is almost three years old). I have walked this one out on many levels. I know that the emotions surrounding an unplanned pregnancy are very real and deeply painful. I know because I have held many precious babies while weeping over them; they are valuable and a blessing.

Having personally faced this situation along with a multitude of times sitting with young people and families who are facing the decision of life or abortion, the argument in that moment sounds nothing like the argument you hear on Sunday morning news shows or around the dinner table. When we hear politicians debate the issue or when our families strike up a conversation at Christmas about who is pro-life and who is pro-choice, you hear arguments like: *It's a woman's right to choose*; *It's her body*; *You can't legislate morality*; *Don't tell me what to do with my uterus*; and *The government should stay out of the bedroom.* The interesting thing to me is that when we sit with the young woman, whether or not she has ever claimed to be pro-life or pro-choice, those are not the arguments that we hear. She says, "My boyfriend will break up with me. My parents will kick me out. I am leaving in a couple of months to go to college. I don't have any money. This is not the situation that a child should be brought into."

Oftentimes, a young woman's circumstances will determine her choice to abort or not. For some, abortion may seem like the only option. Many teens considering an abortion are also considering situations in which they might not terminate their pregnancy.

If I could figure out my finances...

If I could find a way to go to college in the fall...

If someone could help me tell my parents...

...then I would want to carry my baby.

Women who would say they are staunchly pro-choice, with tears streaming down their face are overwhelmed, scared to death, and do not feel like abortion is a good choice for them. Young women committed to Christ sob because they are pro-life yet wonder how they will tell their Christian parents that they have been sexually active and are now pregnant. They are considering abortion, even though it goes against every ounce of their being. Pro-Life/Pro-Choice is a very personal issue and strikes the heart of a woman. People make the choice to abort or carry with a very, very heavy heart.

A parent with a teen facing an unplanned pregnancy feels much of those same emotions. If you are a parent who has waded into the surf with a teen facing a pregnancy, you know that the thoughts that overtake you can be surprising. When our teens find themselves in overwhelming situations, our natural parental instinct is to rescue them at all costs. It can be almost unbearable when they place themselves in a circumstance in which we cannot simply dive in and save them.

So, what do Christian parents do when faced with this situation in their families? What if your daughter comes to you saying she is pregnant or your son, worried his girlfriend might be? What are the steps you go through when swimming in these uncharted waters?

Let's ask the Lifeguards

What do you think about abortion?

I am definitely pro-life. Everything comes down to one basic question: Is it a human being or not? It doesn't matter at that point what the circumstance was surrounding the pregnancy. There are four differences inside/outside the womb: size, level of development, environment, and degree of dependency. You cannot even argue that someone smaller is less of a human. My brother hasn't gone through puberty, so he is less developed than me. Does that make him less human than me? Of course not. Environment: If I go to the moon, does that make me an alien? Or am I a human being on the moon? I am a human being on the moon—environment doesn't make sense as an argument. Degree of dependency: That baby couldn't survive without its mom. Ok, come on now... after birth if the baby doesn't have its mom, will it die? Yes, and that doesn't make them less of a human. We are all dependent on something, and it doesn't make us less human. If babies are human it is murder, period. I can debate this is a classroom or politically, but I wouldn't be good with a person dealing with it. We need people like that (who can deal with those facing the decision). (Jace)

✐ I am pro-life, but the person we are talking to making the decision is also a human being. We have to love the person we are talking to, and we are not in their shoes. It is easy to judge on the outside, but what if it happens to your family? Stating our opinion is important, but being Christians loving the person is more so. Love the person, but hate the sin and the situation. Jace just did work, and I agree totally. But we have to also love the person. (Andrew)

✐ Do we believe what we say we do? We should help those in an unplanned pregnancy see the blessing that the baby will be, why it's worth it. My family has experienced this, and though it was very difficult to walk through, my nephew changed all of our lives. (Christian)

✐ Give common ground and see the person considering abortion as a valuable person. We need to approach things in love because we don't know all that they are faced with. Love the person we are talking to. (Andrew)

✐ People need to be responsible for their decisions. It is irresponsible to choose abortion after you made the choice to have unprotected sex. Abortion should not be an option for people being irresponsible. (Luke)

So many people have had abortions that we are starting to realize abortion is not an easy answer and causes more problems. (Christian)

As a generation, we are winning this one (the debate over the issue of life). Even on a liberal college campus like mine, people will at least respect your choice of being pro-life. The pendulum is swinging in our direction on the pro-life issue. (Jace)

We (my generation) may be more pro-life, but we are also pro-sex. (Andrew)

It was very important to the Lifeguards and to me that we realized the different topics we discussed were more than just discussions. The issues were the very point of pain for people we are in school with, people we pass at the grocery store, even our very own families. Our hearts were full of compassion for those who have swam in these waters. We acknowledged the trails of tears as we passed them, and we expressed thankfulness to the Father, that He makes all things new and there is no sin so "bad" that His sacrifice couldn't cover.

I believe that abortion can feel like the unpardonable sin. If you have a teenager who is wrestling with this decision, my heart is with you. There are plenty of people who will encourage your teen or you as their parent to take the easiest out possible, to choose to end the pregnancy. But believe me, after the decision has been made and the abortion complete, you and your child will feel alone and adrift on the consequences and pain of that choice.

Choosing to carry a child or to abort is life altering. Any decision made will span the course of a lifetime for your teen and for you. For this reason, the Lord tells us that sex and sexuality are sacred. He created sex to be practiced only within the confines of the marital relationship. Marriage is a covenant between a man and woman saying they will be one under the covering of God for a lifetime. Only in that place is it safe for life to be created. Outside of that covenant it is very difficult. It's a sacred place, holy ground, where the Lord meets with the young lady to make a determination of what will happen with that precious, valuable, unique life that has been created. This is no small thing.

My Own Story

My dad was the youth minister of a small Baptist Church where I grew up. I accepted Christ at age five, and I don't remember a time that I did not love Him. I told you in chapter two that I felt a calling of God to serve in ministry from a very early age. But in high school I went through a significant period of rebellion.

I began a relationship with a young man and eventually found myself in an unplanned pregnancy. This young man was not a believer and didn't claim to be. Throughout our relationship, he was behaving the way people who do not have a relationship with the Lord behave. I, however, did know the Lord. I was a believer. I had a strong background in Scripture. I knew Him and that His plans were for good. I knew babies are not a mistake and sex was sacred. I was the one behaving contrary to my heritage and contrary to my relationship with the Lord. Nonetheless, we found ourselves faced with a pregnancy and having to making a decision that would affect us from that point forward. Our choice would mean literal life or death for the child.

The young man said that I could do whatever I thought was best for me and he was going to college and wouldn't be involved. I told my parents, and as you can imagine, there was much emotion and panic. We really withdrew from our community and isolated ourselves from everyone, including each other.

People tend to seclude themselves in the midst of struggle rather than reach out for counsel, because they don't want others to know. Immediately, it becomes a secret. Secrets are kept in the darkness—the enemy's territory. The Lord tells us to bring things into the light. Secrets are dangerous. We had ourselves a secret and were looking for answers. We wanted an answer that would respect our secret and allow us to keep things hidden and out of the light. Panic set in.

Time is crucial for those considering life or abortion. There are no take backs on this one, and the decision affects all involved. In a crisis, we experience a flood of emotion. We quickly move from being afraid to being shameful to being embarrassed to being angry to being insecure and then all over again. We feel things and consider things we would have never dreamed possible.

It isn't necessary that one experience this crisis to relate to the depths of it. Allowing time for emotions to settle, room to see reason, and the patience to listen for that still small voice is vital. Your daughter will likely go from being angry to shameful, scared to excited. Give her the grace of time. Also, allow yourself time to allow your emotions of disappointment, fear, or grief to settle as well. You will get through this, but as you swim for shore on this one, you need to allow yourself a moment or two, which can realistically be a few days, to catch your breath for this swim.

The consequences of my choice still come in waves.

I've literally shared my story hundreds of times, spanning decades, and every time I get the same feeling in my stomach that I felt those many years ago, standing in the drive way telling my dad not only had I been sneaking around dating this guy, but that we had been sexually active and I was pregnant. We told my mom and little sister, and as you can imagine, everyone was shaken to the core. We were all isolated in our own pain.

Isolation is a tactic of the enemy to keep up in darkness so that we weaken. As the Church Body, we are dependent on community for insight and guidance. In the midst of a week's time, because we did not seek counsel, because we were afraid, because we didn't give ourselves time, and because we did not trust the Lord, my family and I decided I needed to have an abortion. Seven days after finding out I was pregnant, my father and I sat in the waiting room of the abortion clinic.

The most alone I have ever felt in all my days was sitting in that waiting room, surrounded by more people than I could count. We were all there together, for the same thing, but we were all completely alone. My dad would tell you the thought that overtook him was, "Our situation is different, but how can *you* people do this?"

Justifying what we know to be sin. ***Believing that, in this scenario, for us, just this once, the rules are different and the boundaries are blurred.*** You think things like, "The Lord says that life is valuable and precious. He ordains life. Yet, in this situation maybe even He can understand why we would do such a thing."

Upon exiting that clinic, I remember thinking; *I can never speak of this again. This is done, I will bury it. I will not look back; I will shut off this pain.* So, I became completely numb.

Emotions are funny little things. You can't choose to feel the good feelings and not the bad. It's all or nothing, on or off. At that point, I was in such emotional pain and turmoil that I just shut down my emotions altogether. Felt better that way. My parents nearly divorced as it sent our family into a tailspin. My poor younger sister was left to her own devices, because I had sucked all the life out of our home.

About two years later, I was desperate, maybe not suicidal, but certainly ambivalent to life or death. Out of hopelessness, I attended a Bible study for women who had experienced an abortion. During this study I began to breathe again. I cried a lot too, but I remember the first few times I was able to actually breathe in—not just oxygen, but the truth of all the choices I had made. I was finally able to breathe in the gravity of my sin. It was painful. Oh, was it. But these were the first laborious steps toward freedom. Freedom from the darkness.

The first steps out of the darkness took my eyes some time to adjust, but I could feel the warmth of the Light, and I could see

Hope in the distance. There was Him. He didn't run from me and He wasn't overwhelmed by my disgusting, dark sin. He offered to wash me and make me new. I had to hold up to Him my filthy, broken heart...but He is gentle and kind and powerful. He made it better. He heals all things. (1 Peter 2:24)

Abortion isn't unforgivable; it's just irreversible. God doesn't change the ending. He allows us to choose, yet He has this way of reworking the story to turn what the enemy intended for our defeat into a beautiful, hope-filled story that points others to Him.

My daughter, Jessica Renée, was aborted in April of 1992. I never took her to kindergarten or taught her to tie her shoes or to count. I never watched her learn how to ride a bike or clean up the skinned knee she earned in the process. Never helped her with her math homework or sat up late with her when she didn't feel well or was afraid of the dark. I didn't get to see her walk out of the DMV waving a driver's license or cry as she walked across the stage at her high school graduation. I will never help her choose a wedding dress nor watch with thankfulness as she becomes someone's wife.

In that sense, for me, it is too late. But the beautiful redemptive nature of the Lord says that there are girls every day facing the exact same decision and our work, our stories, our ideas, and our words can impact them. He says it's not too late for them. It is my prayer that there will be many young women, men, families, and children saved from this horrible pain, from this horrible decision that is life-ending for a child and life-changing for everyone else involved.

As parents, we would do anything to spare our children pain. I encourage you, the mother or father of a teen considering life or abortion, to do all you can to support them in a choice that will bring life. If your son is facing becoming a teen dad, help him to make the difficult choices the will affect the life of the baby and the young lady carrying it. If you are the parent of a soon-to-be teen mom, encourage her that she can have her baby and that she will be glad she did. The only decision that must be made in those first few days following a positive pregnancy test is whether or not your teen will carry the baby. The decision on whether they will parent or place their baby with a loving family through adoption will be made over time. As a parent of a teen in this circumstance, you may feel overwhelmed, like you're caught in a riptide. You might start thinking that you need to know which room to put the baby in, where they will attend kindergarten, and who will pay for their college education before your teens have even gone to their first doctor's appointment. Slow down. You have time to make those decisions. Take it one wave at a time.

Treading Tips

When your teen is facing a life-altering crisis, you consider things you would have never dreamt to be an option. Give the waters time to recede. It feels like a flood, truly. You will experience every emotion you can imagine. Allow yourself time, space, and grace to take on that twenty-foot squall and catch your breath. You do not have to act immediately. Once the water calms, you will be able to think more clearly. When the crashing blows of those initial waves tame a bit, you will be able to hear Him more easily.

You are not a failure as a parent. I have always believed that our parenting is an act of worship on our part. If we parent from a place of being obedient to the Lord and making decisions that we feel convicted and lead by Him to make, then we leave the decisions our children make up to them. It really is, at that point, between them and God. I have had so many parents completely broken in my office say, "I feel like it is my fault. I should have talked with them more or said no to this or that." I will almost always turn to their teen and ask, "Did you know sex outside of marriage was wrong? Did you know that the Lord tells us sex is a covenant and meant to be shared only with our husband or wife?" They always answer, yes. It isn't that they needed one more talk from the right person who would say all of the right things. It is a heart condition. Moms and dads, you can't take all of the blame.

Get help. Go and talk to someone at your local pregnancy center. Talk to your pastor or your youth pastor. Talk to friends who may have experienced this before. It is important to seek godly council. You need help sorting through the decisions that lay ahead. At our office, each morning, I ask the Lord to help us push back the chaos for the families we serve just enough that they have a safe, quiet space to think, to listen for His voice, and to take their first steps.

There is time. You do not have to be able to map out the next eighteen years of this unborn child's life immediately. You cannot know what lies around each turn. Don't try and figure out where they will attend kindergarten or college. All of that will come in time. In the early days, all we really need to decide is whether or not we will choose to give this baby life. Your teen has nine months to make a final decision on parenting or adoption, and then all the other decisions can be made in step.

Here's the hard part: don't rescue your teen. Sure, it is hard to see them sinking. They will struggle and even appear to be drowning. But they develop keen eyesight when they have to squint to see what is coming in the distance. They will see Him. He is not in a hurry and is never late. He is complete peace and has all the answers. When the waves rise we will see Him, if we look. He will meet us; He will meet them, in the midst of the storm, and as long as we don't get in His way. Pray for them. Support them. Love them. Help them. But leave the rescuing to the Savior.

Pregnancy Centers do an amazing work. In our centers, 90% of women considering an abortion will choose life for their children after an ultrasound. This only speaks of the great hope we have in Christ. He can save and He does rescue. Often times it is simply the picture of that sweet baby sucking its thumb, tucked away in the sanctuary of the womb, or the promise that we will be there to support them with clothes, diapers, and formula, or just a prayer and a smile offering hope for tomorrow that affect the women who come to us…a life preserver thrown into the turbulent seas does it's job. It pulls a woman into shallow, calm water where she can once again gain her footing.

Life Preservers

Before I formed you in the womb I knew you, before you were born I set you apart; I appointed you as a prophet to the nations.

Jeremiah 1:5

For we are God's handiwork, created in Christ Jesus to do good works, which God prepared in advance for us to do.

Ephesians 2:10

I praise you because I am fearfully and wonderfully made; your works are wonderful, I know that full well.

Psalm 139:14

But when God, who set me apart from my mother's womb and called me by his grace.

Galatians 1:15

Children are a heritage from the Lord, offspring a reward from him.

Psalm 127:3

In him we have redemption through his blood, the forgiveness of sins, in accordance with the riches of God's grace.

Ephesians 1:7

And all are justified freely by his grace through the redemption that came by Christ Jesus. God presented Christ as a sacrifice of atonement, through the shedding of his blood—to be received by faith. He did this to demonstrate his righteousness, because in his forbearance he had left the sins committed beforehand unpunished—he did it to demonstrate his righteousness at the present time, so as to be just and the one who justifies those who have faith in Jesus.

Romans 3:24-26

Communication

If I could talk to my parents about anything, it would be about my mistakes and struggles. I just want to hear what they have to say. I just need advice and encouragement.
Jace Bennett

Teenagers can be prickly. They are oftentimes uncomfortable with communication because they are still learning how to do it. I know that my teens have trouble articulating their feelings sometimes; they simply don't know what makes them behave a certain way or why. Communicating with teenagers can be painful sometimes too. As a parent, you often must make yourself vulnerable first. Remember that I mentioned parenting isn't for the faint of heart? At this point, we are swimming in deep waters. So, take in a good, long, deep breath. We may go deeper before it gets easier.

So, what do you do when your teen hits the stage of the slight nod, grunt, or "stuff" reply? Communicating with our teens is not always as easy as it would seem. Being on your toes and looking for new and unique ways to bring about good communication will certainly save us from difficulty down the road.

I asked the Lifeguards what the most effective mode of communication is between them and their parents. With only one exception, the Lifeguards responded that face-to-face communication was the most effective. One young lady stated that she was more comfortable communicating in writing such and via text message. The reason she provided is noteworthy: her thoughts are better communicated without interruption when presented in writing. Her response was a heads-up for me, as I am the worst about trying to complete my kid's thoughts. (Though, I am making a sincere effort to allow my teens to speak for themselves and hold any response until they are finished.)

Isn't it interesting that the group almost unanimously agreed face-to-face communication is most effective? Haven't we been told, and possibly believed, our children don't want to hear what we have to say? Well, it turns out they desire direct confrontations with us.

According to a 2008 study conducted by the Dove Self Esteem Fund, the top wish among all girls is for their parents to communicate better with them, which includes more frequent and more open conversations as well as discussions about what is happening in their own lives.[15] Our kids not only desire to talk with us, they desire us to talk with them. Not only is this open communication necessary for a healthy family, it is our children's wish as well.

Communication is priceless and lovely, but certainly not always pretty. In the middle of working on this chapter, I simply bowed my head and asked the Lord what He would like me to pen regarding communication. As I waited on His divine response, images of my own communication with Him over the course of my lifetime flashed through my thoughts, one after the next. Times as a child, when I would pray on my swing set in the back yard, imagining that if I kicked hard enough maybe my toes could touch the floor of heaven. Times as a pre-teen, asking the Lord to give my teammates and I the win, even though I was quite sure He loved the players of the opposing team equally as much as He loved us. (Therefore, I often threw in the fact that I would keep it between us if He would give us just grant that extra finesse on the final hit to pull it off.) I remember a time, as a very broken and desperate teen, driving around in my car late at night screaming at Him through sobs, "Will this pain ever go away? Am I really crazy?" I saw images of myself thanking Him, the night before I would marry my Mr. Gibbs, for His unbelievable faithfulness. Images of my late night talks with Him about His plans for my newborns as I rocked them—the image of an occasional tear on their resting face, which caused them to wiggle their noses, also came to mind. As I raise teenagers who I love more than life, I saw images of me literally on my face in moments of heaving sobs unable to utter a word, yet in deep communication with my God.

The point is that communication isn't easy. Communication isn't easy with the Lord, with our spouses, and it certainly isn't easy with our teens. We can't lay out a plan that can be followed in step. Communication occurs during times of elation and peace but also in times of tears, fear, anger, and despair. Yet, communicating in any circumstance—having the nerve to stand face to face with another and take time out of our busy lives to address what is going on in this relationship, says, "I love you enough. You matter to me."

Let's ask the Lifeguards

What do you feel is important for parents to know about communicating with teens?

I communicate well with my parents because they create quality time with me. My dad has three daughters, and we each get a Saturday where he takes us to breakfast and sits down and we just talk and he challenges me or tells me what he is thinking about me. The fact they made quality time meant a lot. (Stephanie H.)

I always feel free to talk to my mom, and I think that's because I don't feel judged. She will think of examples in her life and it is nice to know that I am not alone. Also, my parents don't hesitate to say they are sorry and that is a big thing for me. (Kaylee)

It is hard for me to communicate with my parents (verbally). It is hard for me to communicate with people in authority over me. Being out of the house has helped. I have trouble articulating my thoughts. It is easier for me to write in a notebook or in a text. I process better. (Paris)

Look for opportunities to have open and intimate conversation with your children. Parents ask for opportunities but often overlook them; these chances will pass you by. (Andrew)

When Tanner was thirteen or fourteen, I could not wait to see him at the end of the day. I believe he might refer to those times (lovingly, I'm sure) as "twenty questions." I couldn't wait to hear whom he sat with at lunch, how he did on the math test, or how his teacher was feeling after being ill. However, this was not Tanner's idea of a peaceful ride home.

Often times when parents want to talk, it's not a time that our kids are ready to be open and honest. Typically, either the ride home from school or sitting at the dinner table are times we want to hear from our teens. However, they will likely be ready to spill the beans when you are getting ready for a long, relaxing bath or to hit the hay. Parents need to be willing to talk when our teens are ready to talk. It may be 2:00 a.m., but if that is when they're ready to open up and share with you, jump on it!

I remember many midnight talks with my dad. Growing up, my dad was the type of parent who didn't care what time of day or night it was, if my sister or I wanted to sit down and talk, he was available. It wasn't always convenient for him, and oftentimes he'd rather be sleeping or working around the house, but he always made time for us. Time is so very valuable. When your teens are open, when they reach out to you, it's a gift.

Creative ways to connect with your teen

During a season of seeking wisdom, I remember asking the Lord for ideas on how to connect with one of my kids. One morning, a crazy idea entered my mind, and I decided to try it. I put a note on my son's pillow inviting him to nachos at 2:00 a.m.! I set my alarm and began making the midnight snack. There are no words to describe the joy in this mom's heart when I heard his alarm begin to beep. We sat in the kitchen, laughed, and shared nachos. There was no need to talk about his grades or the issues we were having. We simply shared time together.

I have heard it said that children spell love, T-I-M-E. I can vouch for that. My son and I did the same kind of thing several more times throughout the course of his teen years. Now, my other two children enjoy our mid-night times together as well. We have put blankets in the dryer to warm them up and then laid on the front yard in the middle of the night, looking up at the stars and discussing what an amazing God we have that He would create such a beautiful night sky, and we stayed up drinking hot chocolate and playing card games. During each of these times, we didn't solve the world's problems. Actually, we didn't even solve our own problems, but my kids will look back on their life and know that their mom was willing to do anything for moments alone with them—simply because I love them. Your children desire the same thing. They need moments alone with you just because you love them.

Another creative way that Brian and I connect with our kids is to take them on dates. Brian takes Madi, and I take the boys. What wonderful times together! We never have to sit down and say, "ok, we are down to ten minutes. Really level with me—we need some deep communication," but every time we have gone on a date with our kids, we have had profound talks. It's because they know we're focused on them and they know that we want to hear what's going on in their lives. They treasure those moments. You will never regret taking your child on a date, and they will treasure the time spent together.

A final idea is to journal back and forth. Several years ago, I bought each one of my children a journal. I write something to them and leave the journal on the end of their bed, and then they write back and leave the journal in my room. This exchange occurs several times each month, and some incredible conversations have taken place on paper. Sometimes we talk about very important things. I will write to them if I know they are struggling with something or if they are having trouble in a certain subject or with a friend. However, sometimes I'll share scripture that I've been praying over them. I've also asked them questions like, "When you go off to college and come home for a holiday, what is your favorite meal that you would want me to cook?" I have enjoyed the answers to those kinds of questions as much as any. (It doesn't always have to be serious and heavy.) Oftentimes, it is through laughter I respond back to them. But we are still building and maintaining a relationship.

I expected that my daughter would love to do the journaling. She is very verbal and open with her emotions. I love that about her! However, I wasn't sure how the boys would respond. To my surprise, they have enjoyed the journaling at least as much as Madi. Because I don't interrupt them, they are able to get their feelings out in writing. I am then free to respond. What a precious exchange this has been! I believe our journaling has been very special for each of my children—allowing us to share deep thoughts and feelings sprinkled with laughter and silliness.

Journaling is a beautiful way to communicate and create memories. Also, what an amazing gift that would be to have a journal you shared over the years with one or both of your parents! Wouldn't that be something to cherish?

Learn to speak their language

The bottom line is that you need to find a way to connect with your child. Often times, boys communicate better with their hands busy. If you have a son take him outside to work in the yard, throw the baseball, or run around the block. Be active and he will be more likely to share. And remember, those boys don't like 20 questions. I literally find myself prioritizing my questions for Jake each day. A young lady is more likely to be the kind to sit down on the couch or at the dinner table with you and open up. Or maybe she is just like our young lady in the college group who needs to write things down. Allow her to do that in a journal.

Relationships are unique, not all teens relate the same way as others. Your relationship is unique with each one of your children.

Make the time to know them and stay connected to them. Don't allow friends, school activities, or anything else to steal your time with them. Time moves so quickly, and you'll not want to look back and wish you had done things differently. In order to communicate, we have to be together. We have to create time and space for our families to talk, and we need to be intentional about not letting the distractions of busy schedules, technology, and outside influences catapult us into the growing demographic of families that spend less and less time as a unit.

How much is TMI when it comes to my past?

Should I share regrets from my past with my teenager? As I've pondered the relationship between parents and teens, as well as communication between the two, honesty finds its way into my thoughts over and over again. It is critical that we are honest with one another. The Lifeguards and I discussed many different topics surrounding this very issue. One of the questions I posed was, "Should parents be open and honest about their own past with their teens?" I was surprised by some of the comments and I believe you will be as well. Many of the Lifeguards believed that parents *should* be honest about their past mistakes. However, most of them also felt it important for parents to clarify that they *regretted* their decision and would choose differently today.

Much of the discussion went to parents who present past poor behavior as a "bragging right" in order to be liked by their teenager and peers. Jace told us that he had a friend whose dad would tell them crazy stories about when he was a teenager, like running from the police and getting in fights. Then he would add, "but you guys don't do anything like that." Unfortunately, Jace's friend has tried to impress his dad by making some wrong decisions. He thought his dad would think he was "cool," but he ended up hindering his future. Not one of the Lifeguards felt this kind of interaction was profitable. The students felt it necessary to ensure the shared information didn't somehow give the teen license to make bad choices as well. The consensus was that past mistakes shared in such a way as to demonstrate repentance and the redemptive work of the Lord in the parent's life was very beneficial.

Let's ask the Lifeguards

Do you feel like parents should be open with their teens regarding their own past?

My parents have been very open and honest with me. That makes it impossible to use that against them. I understand what I will struggle with if I fall to certain temptations. (Stephanie H.)

My mom was super open with me. I think there is a time and a place for it. You don't have to do it right off the bat, my mom waited until I had a relationship with Christ. When my mom opened up to me, it changed the way I viewed my mom and opened up lines of communication. I appreciated her being open and honest. (Layne)

It is much easier to be open with our parents when they are open with us. When we can tell that they are hiding something, it is easier for us to hide things. Being open is important. (Christian)

Kids look up to their parents. I really respect my dad and his walk with the Lord. I saw them (my parents) as larger than life. They have walked with Jesus for so long that, when they will share struggles with us, it helps us know it isn't a snap of the fingers; it is a process. They were open but said, "I will tell you when you're older." They shared more with me at the end of high school. (Andrew)

Sometimes dads will share with their son about all the women they have had and are looking for approval. That is never good. (Luke)

The Lord prepares our heart to hear the things our parents need to share with us. (Layne)

Parents need to be intentional (about creating times to communicate) though, because I learned things at school that I would have rather heard from my parents. (Stefanie P.)

My parents waited to tell me some things until I got older and out of the house. They told me how they used to be. Holy cow, they changed so much for me. Man, even the stuff I am messing up in, they were way worse than that and now they are the best people I know. They became people to me and not just my parents. (Jace)

When our parents show their faults I don't feel so much like I have to be perfect. (Christian)

Battles are won in the light

My dad, my family, and I decided abortion was the answer because we didn't want anyone to know about my pregnancy. It was a secret. Thus, the reason we have made the commitment to now have no secrets in our family. When things are a secret, they have power over you and the enemy can use those things as blackmail. However, when things are brought into the light, he has no more power and an amazing, miraculous thing happens. When the power and the presence of God fall onto our past sin and our shortcomings, it changes everything.

Brian and I together have decided we will not keep secrets in our home. The way we have approached difficult topics, especially pertaining to our pasts, is to be honest when the topic presents itself. Many of us have made mistakes in our past and do not want our children to repeat those same mistakes. We carry a concern of how we will address this with our teens when the time comes. The time to share does come and it comes naturally. You don't need to designate a time when you will just spill your guts about the things that have happened in your past. Thank heaven for that! You will have plenty of opportunity by simply living life to be open and honest in your communication with your teens about past mistakes. Be sure to share the lessons you learned through those mistakes.

I have a few critical issues from my past (described in other chapters) that I was very afraid to share with anyone, but especially with the man I would one day marry and my children.

Is there any past sin that still grips you? Something you fear people finding out about or feel overwhelming shame in remembering? I encourage you to find someone to talk to about it. Choose someone who will point you in the right direction through the scriptures. Admitting my sin absolutely changed my life and the meaning behind the things that I do. I celebrate that today. There is something powerful about just saying out load that you made the wrong choice. In my case, I willfully choose a sinful, destructive path, yet when I talked it out with the Lord and repented, He forgave me. Christ forgives, but confessing our sins to other believers brings healing.

Therefore confess your sins to each other and pray for each other so that you may be healed. The prayer of a righteous person is powerful and effective.

James 5:16

When we confess our sins to other people, safe people, it breaks the enemy's power to blackmail us with our past by bringing it into the Light. When the Light touches our darkness, it transforms our mistakes into something beautiful God can use for His glory. Though I would make some different decisions if I had the opportunity to do it over again, I treasure the lessons I learned. I learned that there is no place you can go where He is not there. I learned for myself that Christ loved *me*, that He died to save *me*, and that *I* desperately needed a Savior. I learned that I was still valuable to Him and that, if I would allow Him, He would turn my despair to joy and use it to point people to freedom. I was absolutely unworthy of all of it, but the price Jesus paid was more than enough. I have since had appropriately-timed conversations with all three of my children about the things in my past. They have asked questions, discussed, and dealt with my past sins.

Believe me, I understand that it is no small thing to have these kinds of discussions, but keeping a deep secret, like my abortion, feels like suffocating.

Have you found yourself in a moment when it seems the world stops, looks your way, and there you stand? Guilty and exposed. Your secret has been found out, and now your fear is replaced by shame as you look into the devastated, disappointed, tear-filled eyes of your family, your friends, your neighbors, and those who love you. I have. I was so ashamed of myself and my sin. I was embarrassed and had no idea what to say, much less what to do. I've stood in a surreal moment when my whole world stopped and turned its head my way, and there was nothing to say. Still, I remember being surprised by my ability to take a long, deep breath. At least for that moment, the suffocation subsided and I began to breathe in and out, in and out...no more secrets.

Having to face your past is never easy. You were deceived and trapped. There is simply one way out. You lay down your ugly truth and you look at it and that probably means people around you will have to look at it, too. But you will be able to breathe again. All is in the open. No more fear, no more shame. You see, *caught* is so good, because on the other side of *caught* is freedom, peace, joy, restored relationships, and hope.

Part of the fear of being open with our teens about our mistakes and regrets is birthed out of the fact that we haven't really come to terms with those choices in our own hearts. Maybe it is time for you to have one of those on-your-face-sob sessions with the Father over your past hurts and regrets. He can take the anger, the brokenness, and the tears. You only need to offer them up to Him. When you are able to be honest with yourself, you've won the battle over the fear of talking to your teens. Prisoners make excuses for their chains; freed men must first repent of their failures so that they may appreciate their pardon.

Honesty Works

It is important for parents to be honest with their teens for a few reasons. One reason is because, unbeknownst to us, our teenagers begin to develop the idea that we are "perfect." They feel as though we've never made a mistake or faced the difficult choices and temptations that they are facing. They feel as though we cannot relate to them. This is simply not true; however, it appears to be true when we try so hard to hide our mistakes. Once you appear to be perfect, you become unapproachable to your teenager.

For we do not have a high priest who is unable to empathize with our weaknesses, but we have one who has been tempted in every way, just as we are—yet he did not sin. Let us then approach God's throne of grace with confidence, so that we may receive mercy and find grace to help us in our time of need.

Hebrews 4:15 – 16

Our teenagers need to feel this same way about us. If we are not honest about our past, if we are not honest in our communication, they will not feel as though they could approach us in their time of need.

Secondly, honesty with our teens is important because we want them to be open and honest with us about their own struggles. How can we ask our children to come to us with difficult issues, to talk to us about their struggles, if we are not willing to be honest with them about our own? We must be the example. Our children learn from what we do, not necessarily what we say. I encourage you to be open with your children. When an opportunity to share presents itself, when they come to you and ask a question, that is a beautiful open door to share some of your own struggles, take it. Don't stop with simply sharing your failures; explain to them what the Lord taught you and how the Lord has used all of those things for good.

As it is important for parents to be open and honest in communication with their teens, it is important for teens to be open with their parents about the struggles facing them. If we as parents don't take the first step in being vulnerable, how can we expect our children to be open and honest with us? Christian, one of our Lifeguards told me, "It is easier to be open with our parents if they are open with us. Honesty builds trust...but wait for the right time, place, and maturity level."

Have you ever watched a little child playing basketball or soccer score a goal for the opposing team? Everyone wonders, "whose team is that kid on anyway?" I know I've thought that in my own family. There is something beautiful about sitting down with our children and just taking time to regroup. Reminding our kids and ourselves that we love each other through our struggles is powerful. We all want to follow Him. We are on the same team. Our family is a team.

In order to be an effective parent, we need good information about the circumstances our teens face. It is important we require our children to be honest with us. Learning to communicate well is very important.

Treading Tips

Allow your teens to speak for themselves. Try not to interrupt or fill in their gaps.

Look for opportunities to have open communication and take them. Create time. Get creative. Nachos at 2 a.m.!

After school or dinnertime may not be the best time to talk with your teen. Talk when they are ready.

Date your kids. Alone time is precious time. Make it count!

Build relationship through journaling. Share a journal and be consistent.

Oftentimes, boys communicate better when their hands are busy – throw the football, work in the yard, paint...but talk!

Find out how your child communicates best. Remember, it costs to communicate.

We are dependent on information. We need the truth in order to be effective with any advice given or decisions made. Honesty must be expected of our teens.

We need to be able to trust one another. If your teenager comes to you and shares something, don't go tell your friends. You should keep things in confidence when possible. I am not talking about keeping things from your spouse, however. Too often one parent keeps things from the other—this is unhealthy and is not good for you family. Both parents deserve the opportunity to have input into the life of their teen.

Spend time together. It is the only way to have a relationship. The more distance you allow between yourselves, the more assumptions are made. Teens assume their parents don't understand them. Parents assume their children don't care what they have to say, and it creates a vast distance between the two. It is important to spend time together as a family. Make memories. Time is important.

We as parents must deal with the shame and regret over our own past so that we can be open and honest about it with our teens.

When sharing about regrets in your life, be sure to share the ways in which the Lord has used those things for His good.

We don't want our teens to view us as perfect and, therefore, unapproachable.

If we communicate with open honesty, our teens are more likely to do so as well.

Life Preservers

The Lord would speak to Moses face to face, as one speaks to a friend. Then Moses would return to the camp, but his young aide Joshua son of Nun did not leave the tent.

Exodus 33:11

My dear brothers and sisters, take note of this: Everyone should be quick to listen, slow to speak and slow to become angry

James 1:9

From the fruit of their mouth a person's stomach is filled; with the harvest of their lips they are satisfied. The tongue has the power of life and death, and those who love it will eat its fruit.

Proverbs 18:20-21

Mentoring

Remember that mentor leadership is all about serving. Jesus said, "For even the Son of Man came not to be served but to serve others and to give his life as a ransom for many." (Mark 10:45)
Tony Dungy

There is such value in having someone who is a little further down the road than you speaking into your life. I believe this to be true for us as adults and parents and for our teens as well. The benefit of this kind of a relationship was very apparent in our time with the Lifeguards. A few of them have a mentor they feel an intimate, strong connection with; some had a bad experience with someone whom they considered to be a mentor; and others never had a mentor but desired one. No matter what experience they had, they all agreed that mentorship was a vital part of one's spiritual walk.

This concept of mentor relationships is biblical and is part of God's design for life and ministry. In scripture, we continually see examples of encouraging, mentor-like relationships. Elizabeth and Mary in Luke 2:39-45; Moses and Joshua in Numbers 11:28 and Deuteronomy 31:14-29; David and Jonathan in Samuel 18:1-4; Paul and Titus in 2 Corinthians 8:16-24; and Naomi and Ruth in Ruth 1:6-22.

I encourage you to spend time reading over these biblical examples of mentorship. Study how they look, what they value, how they encourage and teach each other.

But Ruth replied, "Don't urge me to leave you or to turn back from you. Where you go I will go, and where you stay I will stay. Your people will be my people and your God my God."

Ruth 1:16

In this story we see a relationship in which Naomi teaches Ruth about God, helps her understand a new culture, encourages her to grow in her self confidence, and provides her with life skills, such as how to respond in conflict. Don't we want these same qualities developed in our own teens, or any young person God has brought into our lives?

Mentor relationships are about passing the baton. When I think of those precious teens and young adults whom the Lord has allowed me the privilege to serve, my own children included, I am brought to tears. Those relationships mean the Lord will allow me to plant seeds in them and water those seeds so that, long after I am gone, they will produce a harvest in His Name. Mentor relationships can be for a season or life-long, and each serves its own unique purpose.

Certainly, as their parents, we are our teens' first mentors and will continue in that role throughout our lifetime. As you will see from some of our Lifeguards' comments, their moms and/or dads greatly impacted their lives. This is wonderful, but it is important that other adults have influence with our teens as well. Teens often receive the same truth that we as their parents communicate in a whole new way and with a much more open heart from someone else that they respect. It is important that the adults who have sway with your teen have the same core principles as that of you and your family, but what a valuable resource.

Let's ask the Lifeguards

Why is mentoring important? What impact has it had in your own life?

My sister has been a mentor for me. She disciples me and holds me accountable. We went to breakfast every Friday, and it always ended in prayer and her asking me how I was doing. She had a way of knowing my heart and she knew when I was struggling. I can tell her anything and she encourages me. (Layne)

✒ My mom has always been my mentor, but I also think it is important to have someone outside of your family because they have different experiences. My youth sponsor was my mentor and she was there for me in all situations and having that was a rock for me to stand on. (Kaylee)

✒ There is a girl just a few steps ahead of me in life. She is experiencing the things I am experiencing. She is genuine and open and she wants real answers. (Christian)

✒ My dad is my mentor. He is the analogy master. He says it in ways that you think, *wow, I have never thought of it that way*. He has been the biggest influence in my life by far. He has given me everything I need, and he is the best at it...it is the Joel International Version (JIV). (Jace)

✒ I don't have a mentor. I have prayed for it, but it has never happened. I know I need one. (Paris)

✒ My father was my mentor. In college I faced a lot of trials, and I trusted a Christian man who was a part of a Christian organization on campus. I was leading a bible study and leading people on the team and this man wanted more from me. I think he saw it as a tool for his ministry, but I didn't have more of me to give him. He didn't receive me saying I didn't have more to give, and it ended up where I felt like he was gaining from me. It gave me anxiety to try and live up to my mentor's expectations. (Andrew)

✒ If you are being poured into, it is important to turn around and pour into someone else as well. It isn't fair to take wisdom and pouring into unless we turn around and pour it out. (Christian)

Seasonal Mentor Relationships

Seasonal mentor relationships are often a short-term commitment facilitated by or related to a program or a group. The first curriculum the Lord allowed me to write, *Pearls*, incorporated seasonal relationships. *Pearls* is a program focusing on many different relationships that teenage girls encounter and discusses the value of purity. In my city, groups participating in this program meet once a week for a period of time. Each young lady who comes is assigned to a mentor. When we receive all of the registration forms for a new class, we pray over the list of teens and we match them up with a mentor. I believe the Lord uses this relationship over the course of the ten weeks they spend together to impart truth and encouragement to the teen. On occasion, those relationships continue on for years, but it is more common for the mentor and the mentee to bond for the weeks they meet together and then to periodically touch base with one another in the months and years to come. I have seen these types of relationships born out of time my own teenage children have spent at camp with sweet counselors who loved them, with coaches who have lead them, and in youth groups where they are provided an available pastor. The impact these relationships leave on both the mentor and the mentee can last a lifetime, even if the relationship is only for a season.

One young woman whom I had the privilege to mentor in a seasonal relationship is still a beautiful gift to me. I worked with "Liz" pretty intensely for a few years. She was dealing with sexual addiction and rebellion to the 'nth-degree. She broke my heart a hundred times. She was beautiful and talented and wounded and manipulative. During some of our meetings, I think it brought her joy to see if she shocked or hurt me by recounting her most recent sexual escapades with a stranger. I prayed as intensely for this young woman as I have over my own children. Eventually we lost touch, and when our relationship ended, she was no better off than when it began. Years passed, and I thought of her often but was unaware of where she was in her life. Then one afternoon I was having lunch with *my* mentor when she received a text. She said, "We are doing pre-marriage counseling with the most precious young couple. This young woman named "Liz" has stolen my heart."

As we talked, we discovered that this was indeed my Liz, and the Lord had done an amazing work in her life. My mentor had been ministering to her! Liz and I had lunch and she shared with me all that the Lord had done in her life and I was able to meet the man God had chosen for her. It was water to my soul to see that He won in her life. Though our relationship was seasonal, it changed both of our lives for the glory of the Father.

A friend of mine shared that a few weeks ago on a rainy Tuesday night, the flashing lights of her ever-present phone awakened her. The vibrations on her bedside table caused her to feel around and wonder who and why someone would be texting her so late into the evening. Once she was able to first locate her glasses and then the ringing phone, she opened it to read the following text:

> I just wanted to let you know that I've had such an awesome week. I went to a Bible study and met some other girls and they were all so nice and I've been going ever since. I feel like everything I've learned about God and the Bible all clicked and I finally feel a weight lifted off my shoulders and I feel like I finally have a relationship with God! I just wanted to let you know because you have been such a big part in my life and my heart and I love you!

My friend thought for sure it was a dream and twice checked to make sure she was reading the name correctly. It had been four years since she had heard from this young lady whom she had mentored as a high school student and was now a junior in college. My friend had never stopped praying, never stopped being available, and never lost hope for this young woman. You never know the seeds planted or the direction mentorship may lead someone. It may be years before there is fruit, the mentor may never even see it, but the time taken loving someone else and pouring into them is never in vain. The Lord blesses all those who speak His truth and show His grace.

Lifelong Mentor Relationships

Lifelong mentor relationships are a bit different. This kind of a relationship is not a union that another person is likely to orchestrate for our teen or us. The two involved in this kind of a mentorship share things in common. Elijah and Elisha would be a good example of a long-term mentoring relationship.

"When they had crossed, Elijah said to Elisha, 'Tell me, what can I do for you before I am taken from you?'

'Let me inherit a double portion of your spirit,' Elisha replied." (2 Kings 2:9)

I can't explain well enough the value this type of relationship has had in my life. I have a precious friend that the Lord brought to me four years ago. I was in a season of difficulty. I began to ask the Lord for someone whom I could bounce things off of, call and share crazy irrational struggles with—someone that would laugh with me and pray with me. He brought this precious, godly woman to mind. I knew her but certainly wouldn't say we were in close relationship. After really praying it through, I called her and met with her to ask if she would be interested in investing in me. That was a pretty vulnerable thing to do; and believe me, I wouldn't have done it unless I was convinced it was the Lord. She accepted and we have had such a blessed time over the last several years. We have cried together and laughed together. About two years after she and I began to build this relationship, my mother suddenly and very unexpectedly went home to be with Jesus. My sweet friend was literally life to me and, to some degree, filled some of the gaping holes created by my mother's absence. God is so very faithful.

Not only does God's Word reveal to us the power and importance of mentorship, modern-day research has proven that teenagers who have mentors benefit in many areas. We live in an age where about 40% of a teenager's waking hours are spent without companionship or supervision. Mentors provide teens with a valuable place to spend free time. They provide perspective and impart wisdom. According to a Public/Private Ventures study of Big Brothers Big Sisters, students who meet regularly with their mentors are 52% less likely than their peers to skip a day of school and 37% less likely to skip a class. Youth who meet regularly with their mentors are 46% less likely than their peers to start using illegal drugs and 27% less likely to start drinking.

The 2013 study, "The Role of Risk: Mentoring Experiences and Outcomes for Youth with Varying Risk Profiles," examined mentoring program relationships, experiences, and benefits, especially in the context of high-risk youth. Their findings determined the strongest program benefit, and most consistent, was a reduction in depressive symptoms. This is particularly impactful as almost one in four youth reported worrisome levels of these symptoms (struggling with acceptance and self worth).

It is one thing to hear from a parent the importance and value of abstinence and another to see it lived out in a practical way by someone just a little bit older and wiser. Although the studies and research show mentorship's increasing statistical success in areas such as academics and productivity, the Lifeguards shared that mentorship also was strongly connected to their decision and commitment to abstinence and other areas of morality. Luke said it is "important for young people to find an adult that they can confide in—a mentor relationship...either a parent or someone else. You need to be able to be honest and connect. People who are messing around physically do have regrets. You will not regret waiting for marriage." In fact, when asked about what would help keep young people from engaging in pre-martial sex, Luke went straight to mentorship:

> I don't think there's much more that can be said to help young people grasp the concept of celibacy/abstinence, but rather things that can be shown. With all stereotypes and generalizations aside, I have noticed that it is common for young men without a positive male role model or father figure in their lives to struggle with these things.

> Also, young girls with dad issues or major tension and a lack of understanding with their moms tend to fall in that boat as well. People often become vulnerable and resort to "lookin' for love in all the wrong places," as the great Johnny Lee would say. I think putting more of an emphasis on peer-programs, like PALs or Big Brothers Big Sisters, geared toward high school and college students would do a lot of good work. There should be more than just listening to a health teacher discuss STDs or sitting through yet another propaganda-filled slideshow from a local abstinence support organization. Having the opportunity to spend time getting close to a down-to-earth and fun, yet wise and experienced mentor could really help reach young people.

Treading Tips

Help your teen think through people in their life whom they respect and who might be a good mentor for them. Encourage your teen to talk with that adult and ask them if they would be willing to serve them in this capacity.

Allow your teen to be mentored, encourage them to talk with other people.

When you love your child so much, it is easy to want to be involved in all areas of their lives, to step into every dark place, and to desire open communication. However, accept that there may be areas they are more comfortable sharing with others. Trust that another voice may be able to meet them in places that are hard, and support these relationships.

When our children reach a certain age, we have a special "coming of age" dinner for them. Brian invites the men in our life, men we respect and value because of the way they live their lives, to come and offer words of wisdom to our teenagers. We also communicate to our boys that we trust these men and we would be perfectly comfortable with the boys reaching out to them. Also, we have asked these men to help us hold the boys accountable to the commitments they have made and to support them as they continue to become the men God has called them to be. (We will do the same type of thing with Madison.) Giving our teens permission to pursue a mentor relationship may make a connection with a mentor easier for them.

Respect the space they have with their mentor.

Trusting that your child's mentor is centered in the Gospel, give them the space to build a relationship independent of you. There is nothing worse or more destructive than trying to interfere, get information, or challenge the trust being built. Let your teen's mentor know you are always available, and trust they will come to you if needed. In addition, it is important that you know, trust, and respect the mentor your child is confiding in, this is why suggesting adults you trust is a good idea.

Pray for your child's mentor. There is nothing more important than supporting this adult who is taking time out of their life to serve your teen through prayer. You can love both them and your child and greatly bless the relationship by praying over it.

Mentor others. Be mentored yourself. Raise your teens to see mentorship in action. Have a mentor yourself, someone who can meet you in all seasons of life. Find someone whom you can be vulnerable and real with. Create an environment in your family where these sorts of relationships are valued.

Life Preservers

Therefore go and make disciples of all nations, baptizing them in the name of the Father and of the Son and of the Holy Spirit, and teaching them to obey everything I have commanded you. And surely I am with you always, to the very end of the age.

Matthew 28:19-20

Likewise, teach the older women to be reverent in the way they live, not to be slanderers or addicted too much wine, but to teach what is good. Then they can urge the younger women to love their husbands and children,

Titus 2:3-4

Jonathan said to David, "Go in peace, for we have sworn friendship with each other in the name of the Lord, saying, 'The Lord is witness between you and me, and between your descendants and my descendants forever.'" Then David left, and Jonathan went back to the town.

1 Samuel 20:42

Preparing Teens for College & Beyond

What you get by achieving your goals is not as important as what you become by achieving your goals.
Zig Ziglar

I am so thankful for God's Presence. You know, it is so tangible at times. So thick...so thick that it can hold us up—our physical bodies, our emotional needs, and our broken hearts. His Presence sustains us. His Presence is a life preserver in the truest sense of the word. Holding us up when those waves come crashing in on us. Learning to release our teens into a life of their very own sure looks like a larger-than-life wave making quick ground.

That day when we load up our cars and drive our eighteen-year-olds to the college life awaiting them comes all too quickly. Time sneaks up on us. Protecting our teens through high school while preparing them to leave the nest can be tricky and overwhelming. Sometimes the issues that we perceive to be the "big" ones may not be the same ones that seem insurmountable to our children. When talking with the Lifeguards, I asked them many questions about the high school to college transition: what they hoped their futures looked like, what they felt unprepared for, and what their struggles were in college. One of the more surprising parts of our discussion came as we talked about being away at college.

Parents usually assume that when our children leave for school they're going to be so excited about being away from us. Well, that's actually not the case (at least, it wasn't with the Lifeguards). Without exception, all of the Lifeguards wished their parents visited more in college. When they get away in those dorm rooms and they're on their own, so to speak, our teens miss us. They miss the interaction with us. Take the opportunity to text or call to maintain communication. They need it. They love it, even if they don't show it. They value your time; they value you. Our teens know when they're a priority.

Let's ask the Lifeguards

What are the differences between the college life and life in high school?

For me it is the responsibility, vast change of responsibility and independence. You have to answer to parents (in high school). In college you make choices and you don't check in with anyone. You are making your own decisions. You can be better or fall through the cracks. (Jace)

I lived kind of in a bubble, and I was closest to church friends in high school. At college I realized I had to pursue those kinds of friendships (Christian). It just really opened my eyes because I didn't have that easy bubble. I had to pray for them and seek them out. (Layne)

In high school you had buddies; in college you are looking for brothers or sisters. Also, if you are in a dating relationship with a girl or a guy, it is a whole different kind of relationship (in college). You are dating for a purpose and looking for someone to spend your life with. You aren't just working a summer job; you are considering your life's occupation. (Andrew)

I didn't know it was going to be hard to find like-minded Christians in college. (Stephanie H.)

Deeply loving = difficult to release

This is the stage that my family is currently navigating, the transitioning. My oldest son is married and a dad and has just become an airman in the United States Air force; my middle son is in high school and involved in many different activities, sports, and interests; and my daughter isn't far behind.

Since the day my eyes first locked with theirs, I have felt a deep responsibility to guide my children in the way that they should go. Not unlike many of you, I have believed over the years that my children could be surgeons, politicians (yikes!), involved in ministry, astronauts, or members of the armed forces. The sky is the limit. However, there is a phenomenon that occurs somewhere in the journey from childhood to adulthood that many of us have experienced but few discuss.

When my children were young, Madi was about two and Jake four, Madi was sick and needed to go to the doctor. It so happened that Jake had a well-check visit coming up in the next few days, so out of convenience, I rescheduled his appointment to kill two birds with one stone. Jake had endured several earaches etc. in his short little lifetime, and he HATED shots. He used to call them stickers; and when we would head to the doctor, he would say, "I don't want a sticker!" It took me a while to realize that he wasn't talking about the Buzz Lightyear sticker at the checkout counter, but the shot, or sticker as he called it, which actually earned him a Buzz! Anyway, I decided not to tell Jake ahead of time that he would be seeing Dr. Young as well.

When Madison finished with her appointment, it was Jake's turn. The visit went ok, until the doctor said that the nurse would be right in to take care of his booster shot. That's when things went south…"But I'm NOT SIIIIIICK!"

Sometimes that same scenario happens to us in adulthood: We are going along with life by the horns. All systems are a go and life is good. But, unbeknownst to us, we have an appointment for a checkup.

I had a checkup recently when our oldest son, Tanner, joined the Air Force, swore in, and boarded a plan. Now, don't get me wrong, I love this country, and I love and admire our military. I am proud to be an American, and I am so proud of the men and women who protect and defend us. But as a mom, watching *my* son raise his right hand and take an oath, and then watching as he literally steps into a new destiny—if I am honest, it about broke my heart. I had other plans. I wanted him to live ten minutes from me so that I could see my grandchildren a few times a week. My plan was to attend their sporting events and school plays and to have Fab Fridays at GiGi's house. I was comfortable and my plans were safe. My plans were interrupted.

I learned a few things from my unexpected checkup:

1. I learned that our children are only ours for a short time and even then we hold them with an open hand.
2. I learned that just because *the* plan wasn't *my* plan, it doesn't make it the wrong plan.
3. I learned that my son is a man, a man with eternity and adventure in his heart and now is his time to live.
4. I learned once more that, when I prayed for my little boy, God listened. I asked the Lord to protect him and direct him. I asked the Lord to show him the way to go and never let him get too far away to hear His still, small voice. I asked Him to make my little boy a great man.

Well, as I watched Tanner take the first steps toward His calling, I heard that still, small voice say, "I've kept my Word this far, and I don't intend to stop now."

I don't like checkups, but I needed a booster shot. I got one. The Lord reminded me that good enough isn't good enough. We are all called to greatness, to make an impact. I don't like "stickers" either, but I am thankful for the injection of faith and hope I received.

As the beaver in Narnia would say, *"Safe? No, He's not safe. But He's good."*

I love Him, and I love you. I'm asking Him to begin to reveal His calling and purposes for your family. Chase Him. His feet are planted on your land. Join Him.

There comes a point when we mourn the loss of our own hopes and dreams for our children. Some teens go through a time of rebellion and we must reevaluate our plans for their future; however, many teens *do not* go through a time of rebelling, and I certainly do not believe we should anticipate rebellion in our own teenagers. But even when they stay on target, it is likely, as parents, we will find ourselves having to lay down our dreams for them.

I remember a day of deep sobs and much emotion as I asked the Lord to help me with my teenagers. Hearing Him gently whisper to that not only was I not in control, but that I really never was, I began to accept that only the Lord knows the plans He has for my children. It is outside of my control. I began a process of laying down my expectations of their future and mourning the loss of those dreams while taking hope in the truth that His ways are not our ways and that His plans are always greater than ours. I certainly don't have it down, but I am seeking the Lord for glimpses of His callings for my children, and I am praying that they would be strong and prepared in all seasons.

One of the heaviest burdens we bear is for our children. We feel such responsibility. We are responsible for their physical needs being met, for pointing them to Christ, for encouraging their passions, for fostering a healthy relationship with them, for loving them, and certainly there are many more burdens we could add to this list. But one thing occurred to me while pondering my children's futures: I am *not* responsible for their calling, their purpose. Thank heaven. I still have days when I wonder what my own calling is and, especially on those days, I am thankful that our Father has plans. We don't have to be the architects of our teens' futures. Our job is simply to strengthen them spiritually and teach them to love Him first and love others as themselves.

The purposes and callings of our children are not our responsibility. I don't know about you, but that sure relieved some pressure for me. "For I know the plans I have for you,' declares the Lord." (Jeremiah 29:11) It's not for us to research or demand. It's between the two of them. He has a unique plan for each of them, and He's working out His plans. Our part is to teach them to listen for Him. In my mind, God's favorite game is hide-and-seek. He loves thrill and loves to be found. He isn't hiding from us, but He so desires to be sought. Teach your kids to play along.

Callings

God gifts each of us with unique interests, talents, or abilities and then calls us to specific purposes. Callings are not "drummed up." Your calling, your spouse's calling, your children's callings are not something you have to orchestrate. Sure, we need to have a good work ethic. We need to set goals. We need to operate in excellence in all things as a good testimony of the King. But you can't create your own calling or that of those you love. He simply leads us into His plans. Whatever His calling is for your children, He is there. The precious feet of the Dream Giver are firmly planted in the soil of their inheritance, leading them there. The key is to see Him and follow. Simple.

Callings aren't to be compared. As a parent, it is sure easy to see other young people and either compare our children to them or try and discount or diminish their accomplishments to make our children feel better (or us feel better). The fact is the callings of others are to be celebrated, because their greatness does not diminish the callings of our loved ones. Peter asked Jesus about John's calling: "What about him?" Jesus responded, "If I want him to remain alive until I return, what is that to you? *You* must follow me." (John 21:22) He's not forgotten our young ones. He has called them to something great, regardless of what their peers are called to.

Rough waters of change

Those high school and college years can be difficult for parents, but even more so for our teens. Several of our Lifeguards experienced tremendous changes in what they thought were God's plans for them during this time.

Tate was the "big man on campus" in high school. He was a talented athlete in a class of much athletic ability. He was like and respected in his community. It was difficult for him to go from a place where everyone knew him and celebrated his accomplishments to making a new place for himself in college, where he was unknown. Tate experienced firsthand the transition from being a big fish in a small pond to a small fish in a big one, and it was hard.

Christian had her heart set on attending one particular university and pursuing a major that she felt certain was her life's calling. Only days before the deadline to commit, she changed her choice of university (to the largest rival of her childhood choice, I might add), shocking everyone including herself. Not long after that decision, she changed her major as well. Christian has had a very successful college journey, but it didn't look at all like she had expected.

Layne attended one university and felt so out of place and alone. Nevertheless, she liked making decisions on her own and handling situations herself. She transferred her sophomore year of college because she felt the Lord tugging on her heart. Through weeks of prayer and learning how to trust the Lord, she moved near home to the one school she vowed never to attend. Now, Layne believes her transfer was an amazing blessing and she can't imagine being anywhere else. She feels like this decision helped her sort out her priorities. Layne believes learning to listen to the Lord and obey has helped her avoid the frustrations and stress that she used to deal with regularly.

If Jace is anything, he is a Christian, focused, Texas wrestler. Where did the Lord send him? To Cornell in New York State. He has had to stand his ground on so many levels and has experienced a culture much different from his own belief system. But what better training ground for a future attorney? Jace has been entrenched in heated battle and debate over the past few years and has developed strength physically, emotionally, and spiritually. Great training ground, difficult, but great.

And then there is my dear friend, Andrew. Andrew is a giant of a man, inside and out. In 2009 he was awarded the Happy State Bank Overall Athlete of the Year for football and track. He attended OSU as a football player, and his dream was to play in the NFL. Andrew is one of the most charismatic people I have ever met. People are just drawn to him. In high school, he stood out in athletics and as a person. He was an amazing athlete but had also taken a strong stance for Christ by choosing purity in all aspects of his life, and sometimes—many times, that left him standing alone. After many injuries, concussions, and a back surgery at OSU, Andrew found himself having to lie flat on his back for twenty hours each day for six months. He experienced memory loss and had to learn to walk again, and his dream of playing in the NFL became a distant memory. Andrew changed universities and sports, becoming an All-American in track and field at Abilene Christian University, where met his beautiful bride Peyton and just took his MCAT. Would he have ever guessed? Probably not. Did he learn much? Indeed.

Every one of our Lifeguards has a story of changing circumstances that could be shared here. Life is a series of changes; our part is learning to hold plans and people with an open hand, trusting in the faithfulness of the Father. I am so thankful that our steps are ordered of the Lord. Teaching our teens to set goals, work hard to achieve the opportunities ahead of them, and then trust Him if the path takes an unexpected turn is critical.

If you don't know where you are going, how will you ever know when you have arrived?

Let's Ask the Lifeguards

What are the greatest stressors in college?

Being there alone. You left everything and everyone that you know, and that caused a lot of stress for me because I didn't have that comfort. Everything you choose has more meaning, so more stress. (Kaylee)

Immediately I felt a ton of stress like don't screw up, you are an adult now. I felt like I had to be perfect, no redo. (Christian)

My day started early in the morning and it lasted till late at night and I would miss phone calls from my parents and that would upset me. I would stay up late at night and cry because I felt all alone and it was all on me. It took me a long time to get used to it. I am not much of a crier, but I would call my mom at three in the morning wanting to come home. (Tate)

What are common struggles on a college campus that parents should prepare their teens for?

I think for me, not getting in with the party crowd as an attempt to just fit in. (Stefanie P.)

I had a hard time because no one agreed with my point of view. I had no one to rely on. I got kicked out of my first college class. My professor had just talked about evolution for a long time and then started talking about cells. She said, "This cell is designed to..." and I said, "Wait, did you just say that cell was designed?"
"Yes..."

"That's crazy because if something is designed it must have a designer."

The whole class laughed and she freaked out. Then I had no one to talk to about it at night. (Jace)

✒ Loneliness. When you leave home and go to college, you will feel lonely. (Andrew)

How did you hear from the Lord during your time away at college?

✒ The Lord removed me and isolated me so that I could focus on Him. He moved me from one university to another. (Layne)

✒ Before I went, I knew I was going a long way away. I missed my mom when I went to church camps; I was a momma's boy. How was I going to go that far away? My dad told me just before I left for school, "the happiest you will be is inside your purpose, even if it is hard." I reminded myself of that many times. I started trying to look at the positives of everything. Sometimes when you look at it a little differently, it changes things. (Jace)

✒ I am always going, and I am quick to say what God is doing. I don't take time to listen. If I don't listen, then it isn't a conversation; it is a voicemail. That is something I learned, to be still enough to hear His voice. I came from such a conservative place spiritually that listening to the Lord was hard for me. When I would spend time just quiet and meditating on the Word, I felt like it was voodoo or something. But I grew tremendously. (Andrew)

Treading Tips

Give yourself time and space as a parent to grieve how fast the time has flown and the dreams you are laying down for your teen that will not likely be realized.

Lay down the burden of your teen's callings and purposes. Those are between them and the Father. Teach them to listen for His voice and seek Him. He will direct their steps.

Don't fall into the trap of comparing your teen's callings with those of others. They are unique and will make a unique impact on the world.

It is important to set short term as well as long term goals. Short-term goals keep us going. We need to be able to experience small successes along the way toward our life-time goals. It gives us strength to continue on our journey. Help your teen think of goals that they can achieve this school year or over the next six weeks. These goals may or may not be associated with their longer-term goals. But either way, they supply needed encouragement and a sense of accomplishment.

Our teens must be willing to put work into achieving their goals. If they set a "goal" for themselves and then sit back and wait for it to one day miraculously happen, that isn't a goal; it's a wish. A goal is a dream that has been pondered. Time has been taken to think it through, and our teenagers have considered the steps necessary to fulfill it. Then they must get to it! Hard work and persistence do pay off!

It is important to teach our teens to understand their personal strengths as they begin to set goals. Here is a link to a website for your teens. This site will provide a strength finder quiz that is fab-

ulous and will give your teen some insight into what might really interest them.
www.teenmania.com/careers/strength-finders

Life is hard sometimes, and our teens must assume that there will be obstacles. If the assumption is that it will be nothing but smooth sailing when they begin to work toward a goal, boy are they in for a big surprise. There simply *will* be obstacles and distractions. Remind your teen to go in with eyes wide open. Anticipate the obstacles and strategize ways to overcome them. Remember, we are more than conquerors through Him who loves us! (Romans 8:37)

Setting goals and focusing on the horizon is also a way in which we enjoy life. If our teen's focus is on the dust under their feet as they pound out their course each day, they become discouraged and exhausted. But if our young people take time to lift up their heads and focus on their goals in the distance, they will certainly notice the beauty of their surroundings and the pleasure of their traveling partners, as well.

Take the opportunity to text or call your teen or college student to maintain communication. They need it. They love it...even if they don't seem to. They value your time and they value you. Our teens know when they're a priority.

Let's allow our teens to become young adults with callings and aspirations. Even though it is hard for us to release them, we don't want them to feel guilty about pursuing His best for them. Catching and releasing is a good but difficult lesson for parents to learn. (That release part is so hard for me, but so necessary.)

Life Preservers

Fathers, do not exasperate your children; instead, bring them up in the training and instruction of the Lord."

Ephesians 6:4

"Come let us go up to the mountain of the Lord, and to the temple of the God of Jacob. He will teach us his ways, so that we may walk in his paths..."

Micah 4:2

"For I know the plans I have for you," declares the Lord, "plans to prosper you and not to harm you, plans to give you hope and a future."

Jeremiah 29:11

Building an Ark

On that very day Noah and his sons, Shem, Ham and Japeth, together with his wife and the wives of his three sons, entered the ark...Then the Lord shut them in...The waters rose and increased greatly on the earth.
Genesis 7: 8, 13 & 16

Well, we've done it. We may be exhausted, cramped up, and waterlogged...but we have made it to the shore. We swam some miles together and faced some pretty scary waves and sea life. What a wonderful feeling firm ground underneath your feet can be after being tossed to and fro.

This is exactly my prayer for this book, that it would be a firm place for you to stand, a place where you can get your footing and gain some perspective in the midst of all the craziness, sadness, joy, heartbreak, and satisfaction of raising teenagers.

I realize that we did not cover everything like the issues of drugs, alcohol, cutting, and healthy friendships (to name a few), but I believe we covered the issues the Lord asked us to tackle. I don't believe that we can know every challenge that our families will face, but the question remains: When the flood waters come and the seas get choppy (and they will), do we know how to keep our heads above water and throw our children a life preserver?

I can't tell you all of the joy and sadness that our group has faced during the time it has taken to complete this project. Layne and Andrew are both married. Paris has studied abroad, twice! Christian is doing an internship with a large financial firm. Jace has been ranked eight in the country with wrestling and is preparing for law school. Tate is coaching football. Luke is pursuing a film career and on and on and on. Me, I'm still treading right alongside you, raising teenagers of my own. I am speaking and serving and loving being a wife, mom, and Gigi to my sweet grands.

And there has been sadness. As I write this, I am finishing a prolonged time in the mountains putting the finishing touches on all that you just read. The week before coming here was a hard one for me to describe.

Here is a text I sent out to the Lifeguards that will explain:

> Hey, my friends! I hope you are all doing well and having the time of your life! I want you to know that I pray for you almost every day, and I'm cheering so loudly from my seat as I see and hear of you each accomplishing great things in His Name! My heart races every time I think of you and all that you'll do for the Kingdom. I want to give you an update on our book and ask for your prayers. I am in the mountains this week and my goal is to finish my part of the writing. I don't really have words to describe how I am feeling spiritually. Every time I have designated time to work on this project we have faced attack and it has been in every area you can imagine. This time has been no different. Every obstacle you can imagine attempting to get in the way of this time focused on the book has been thrown at us. This week has been the most intense one for me personally I have experienced as an adult. I have been overwhelmed with thoughts of "people think you and all that you stand for is a joke." I can't really explain all of it, and I am trying to battle through...but what I would like to do is give up. I won't do that because I believe in what He's called us to do and this will be such a help and encouragement to families. I believe the Lord wanted me to ask you to pray for the project, pray for the families that will be impacted, and pray for me. I love you so and value your prayers more than you can know. I am so very proud of all of you. Struggle well.

I share that because I want you to truly understand the young people who served you and sacrificed for Him in this project.

A few of their responses:

Layne: "Though the cherry trees don't blossom and the strawberries don't ripen, though the apples are worm-eaten and the wheat fields are stunted, though the sheep pens are sleepless and the cattle barns are empty, I'm singing joyful praises to GOD. I'm turning cartwheels of joy to my Savior God. Counting on God's rule to prevail. I take heart and gain strength. I run like a deer. I feel like I'm king of the mountain!" (Habakkuk 3:17) Praying for you...Run like a deer!

Kaylee: I pray for a mental and emotional hedge of protection over you. That you will see the value of what we are doing and that the thoughts from Satan be removed...thank you for your perseverance.

Stefanie: Thank you for telling us how you are truly feeling! That is being a real Christian! We all experience these rough roads at times, and it's encouraging to hear the truth of the struggle from other Christians because I know we will all get through. There is only a big struggle because the devil can't stand the idea of such a powerful book impacting families. Keep on keepin' on. We've got a powerful God on our side!

Christian: I do not think your mission is a joke. I think it saved me from mountains of heartache that I see my friends experiencing. I want every girl and boy to be able to avoid that pain or be able to heal from it if they have already experienced it. I believe with my whole heart that this book is meant for great things, and I stand behind you, guarding your vulnerable side against the enemy! He comes to steal, kill, and destroy, but we know that our God does immeasurably more than we can ask or imagine! I am with you all the way!

And then Andrew called...

"Mrs. Candy...remember Noah? He built an ark to be a shelter in the storm before it had ever even rained! And it didn't take him a year or two, but 100 years to complete it. We are building an ark, a safe place for families to run in times of trouble, and if it helps only one family, then it was worth all of our sacrifice."

This is my prayer for you: that in your times of trouble, storms, and high seas you would have an ark to run to for refuge. In today's culture, you are fighting against high tide and deep waters to raise teenagers who fear God and seek righteousness. It isn't easy on good days and can come near drowning you on bad ones. But the fact is we serve a God who will never abandon us or allow us to become lost in a sea of trouble. His Word and His precepts are a refuge, a safe place, and an ark where we can protect our families from the onslaught of the enemy.

The Lord commands the oceans. He walks on the water—even the winds and the waves obey Him. Our part is to build the ark, piece by piece, truth upon truth, standard upon standard, to protect our families. Then He will seal it, just like in the days of Noah. He will shut us in and we will be saved.

> *And God said, "This is the sign of the covenant I am making between me and you and every living creature with you, a covenant for all generations to come: I have set my rainbow in the clouds, and it will be the sign of the covenant between me and the earth. Whenever I bring clouds over the earth and the rainbow appears in the clouds, I will remember my covenant between me and you and all living creatures of every kind. Never again will the waters become a flood to destroy all life."*
>
> Genesis 9:12-15

Rescue swimmers must have flexibility, strength, endurance, and...be able to think and perform challenging tasks while submerged...

It is my prayer that when the waves seem overwhelming and the shore appears miles away, you will reach for a few of these life preservers and remember that you are not alone. You and your teen have a Lifeguard just a breath away. Swim.

See you on the beach,

Candy

Endnotes

1.http://www.military.com/military-fitness/coast-guard-special-training/rescue-swimmer-fitness- standards

2.http://www.covenanteyes.com/2010/08/19/teens-and-porn-10-stats-your-need-to-know/

3. Jimmy Evans, 7 Secrets of Successful Families (MarriageToday, 2002).

4. Chiara Sabina, Janis Wolak, and David Finkelhor, The Nature and Dynamics of Internet Pornography Exposure for Youth (pdf), CyberPsychology & Behavior, 2008, (http:// www.unh.edu/ccrc/pdf/CV169.pdf).

5. Rewiring Young Brains, September 9, 2009, (http:// www.pbs.rg/wgbh/pages/frontline/digitalnation/living-faster/digital-natives/rewiring-young- brains.html).

6. Generation M2: Media in the Lives of 8- to 18-Year- Olds, The Kaiser Family Foundation, January, 20, 2010, (http://kff.org/other/event/generation-m2- media-in-the-lives-of/).

7. Mary Madden, Sandra Cortesi, Urs Gasser, Amanda Lenhart, and Maeve Duggan, Parents, Teens, and Online Privacy, Rep. Pew Internet, 20 Nov. 2012. Web. 08 May 2013.

8. Amanda Lenhart, Teens, Smartphones & Texting, PewResearch Internet Project, March 19, 2012, (http://www.pewinternet.org/2012/03/19/teens- smartphones-texting/).

9. http:/en.wikipedia.org/wiki/Ask.fm

10. Chatroulette Is 89 Percent Male, 47 Percent American, And 13 Percent Perverts, TechCrunch blog, March 16, 2010, (http://techcrunch.com/2010/03/16/chatroulette-stats-male-perverts/).

11. Texas attorney general warns parents about video chat site Chatroulette, Dallas News article, November 26, 2010, (http://www.dallasnews.com/ sharedcontent/dws/news/texassouthwest/stories/030810dnnatchatroulette.18a0fb88b.html).

12. Christy Callahan, The 8 Worst Apps for Your Kids, education.com, May 1, 2013, (http://www.education.com/magazine/article/worst-apps- kids/).

13. Generation M2: Media in the Lives of 8- to 18-Year- Olds, The Kaiser Family Foundation, January, 20, 2010, (http://kff.org/other/event/generation-m2- media-in-the-lives-of/).

14. Mary Madden, Sandra Cortesi, Urs Gasser, Amanda Lenhart, and Maeve Duggan, Parents, Teens, and Online Privacy, Rep. Pew Internet, 20 Nov. 2012. Web. 08 May 2013.

15. "Real Girls, Real Pressure: A National Report on the State of Self-Esteem," The Dove Self-Esteem Fund, http://www.isacs.org/misc_files/ SelfEsteem_Report%20%20Dove%20Campaign %20 for%20Real%20Beauty.pdf, (June 2008).

Book Candy Gibbs for your next event.

For more about Candy and her other products, visit:

www.candygibbs.com

Chosen is dedicated to helping 8 to 12-year-old girls live their lives in a way that is honoring and worthy of the Savior, Jesus Christ.

Join Candy as she journeys through scripture to lead your young girls to seek and know the One who chose us! The *Chosen* curriculum includes a Leader Guide, Student Journals, DVD Lessons taught by Candy, and more.

Order *Chosen* today at www.candygibbs.com!

Pearls

Pearls is a biblical approach to abstinence and relationships. It is about purity in every area of life. The Father is calling your daughter to greatness. All the promises the Lord gave you for her are true!

This study includes Mentoring Guides, Teen Study Books, a Parents' Guide, and more! Order *Pearls* today at www.candygibbs.com!

@candygibbsblogs
www.facebook/candygibbs
candy@candygibbs.com